The Sea Wife's Handbook

The Sea Wife's Handbook

by Joyce Sleightholme

illustrated by J. D. Sleightholme

HENRY REGNERY COMPANY · CHICAGO

First published in 1970 by Angus and Robertson (U.K.) Ltd., London
Published in 1971 by Henry Regnery Company
180 North Michigan Avenue, Chicago, Illinois 60601
Manufactured in the United States of America
Library of Congress Catalog Card Number: 72-143860
International Standard Book Number: 0-8092-8862-1

Contents

Foreword

Since the time of Ulysses, sailors have been faced with the problem of what to do with their wives and sweethearts when they go cruising. Although a skipper is sometimes blessed with an able and enthusiastic sea wife, his usual choice lies between leaving a lonely, abandoned spouse ashore or taking her along despite the probability that she will be inept and unhappy. Joyce Sleightholme sets about trying to correct this deplorable dilemma in her excellent handbook for sea wives.

Few women seem better qualified than the author to advise and instruct yachtsmen's wives in the sport of cruising under sail, since Joyce Sleightholme is not only a sea wife of broad and considerable experience, but also a former editor of a well-known yachting periodical. Furthermore, she has had an able assistant and consultant in her husband, J. D. Sleightholme, the book's illustrator, who is himself a boating author and editor of the British magazine *Yachting Monthly*.

Although many sailors with the credentials and experience of Joyce Sleightholme might be unsympathetic with the trials and tribulations of an apprehensive female neophyte, the author instructs with the utmost patience and understanding, as though she vividly remembers her own indoctrination. She assumes the reader has no prior knowledge of seamanship, and the beginning sea wife is introduced to the subjects in easy stages, one step at a time.

From the first paragraph on, *The Sea Wife's Handbook* strikes me as being very well done from the standpoints of style, usefulness, and basic soundness of information. The principles of safety and seamanship expounded are fundamental and universal. Coastal cruising in England, where the author gleaned most of her hard-won experience, is generally more difficult than it is on this side of the ocean. By comparison, popular American sailing grounds are relatively warm in the summer, currents and tides are less extreme on the average, gales are normally less frequent, and most U.S. harbors afford greater protection. Thus it seems reasonable to assume that if happy and competent sea wives can be made in England, American women can even more readily be converted to capable sailing enthusiasts.

Admittedly, cruising in a small sailboat is not every woman's cup of tea, but among those who are determined to become competent sailors, some will truly excel. In fact, the author implies (daringly) that more than a few women have the potential of surpassing their husbands in nautical know-how, although she wisely warns such precocious sea wives against undermining their husband's authority.

Women passengers who are kept nautically ignorant and never allowed to participate in the management of the boat may either grow bored in calm weather or apprehensive in heavy weather during a cruise under sail. On the other hand, a sea wife who is trained and encouraged to take the helm, handle lines, read the chart, and help with the ground tackle or sails will very likely become not only an enthusiastic sailing companion, but a useful crew member and an important factor in the safety of the vessel.

Exactly what is expected of a competent sea wife—proper conduct, necessary knowledge, and required skills—is clearly expressed in *The Sea Wife's Handbook*. Thus, if the reader cannot or will not discourage her man from his seagoing predilection, she most certainly can become a first class sailor herself. In this way she can enjoy her husband's company, learn to appreciate the pleasures of cruising under sail, and be a useful (at times, *essential*) crew member.

Richard Henderson
Gibson Island, Maryland

Preface

There was a time when a woman aboard a yacht was content to be decorative, to get on with her fancy needlework and leave the work to her menfolk and their paid crews. Not any more. Nowadays yachts are tiny by comparison and there just isn't room for dainty passengers.

All the same, there is a surviving feeling that a woman aboard a boat really cannot cope with more than purely domestic affairs —that her place is in the galley, in fact. Admittedly she can make a better job of the cooking than the average male, but in a small family cruiser, where father elects to handle the boat single-handedly most of the time, since there's no alternative, a woman who knows how to throw a heaving line, take a compass bearing, stow a sail, secure a mooring rope, and so on, makes the difference between a small yacht being dangerously undermanned and being adequately crewed. In a real emergency, a woman who can *sail* the boat could mean the difference between life and death.

Sailing is more than a sport, it is a way of life. For growing children it is formative. Just as a woman ashore takes a full part in all the activities of her family, so she can learn to take a fuller part in life afloat. As first mate she is second in command, and the more she learns the better she does her job.

1/Coming to Terms with Yachting

To my mind there are four types of sailing wives: those who sail and enjoy it; those who sail rather than be left behind, and put up with it with bad grace; those who won't sail at any price, try to stop their husband when he goes and are ungracious when he gets back; and those who pack him off with their blessing, then busy themselves with their own hobbies.

The family of the first type is especially lucky. The boat becomes the "weekend cottage," owner and wife sail happily together, she is useful on board, and the children grow up accustomed to weekends and holidays afloat, taking it all in their stride. Soon the lucky owner has trained all his family and the ship runs like clockwork. This is the ideal.

In his own way number four's husband is just as lucky. Not for him family participation, but he finds another sailing enthusiast and sails with an easy conscience knowing his wife is happy in her own interests.

None of us would ever admit to being either of the other two types, but in fact there are thousands of both. Who knows, perhaps when she has enough sailing hours behind her the wife in the second group will like sailing for its own sake? It has happened that way. The main snag is that until she does tackle her fair share of the jobs on board, the boat is not adequately crewed. The owner is virtually single-handed, but without the advantage of complete single-mindedness which most single-handers have. Instead of being able to devote all his attention to sailing his ship he will have half an eye lifted to see what effect the conditions are having on his unwilling crew.

Not so the husband of number three. He can at least put all his mind to sailing while he is afloat. Like number four he will find a regular crew to share the work on board and for him the

Photo: Eileen Ramsey

The *Westerly Centaur*—a typical small family sailboat

boat will be a real retreat. All hell may break loose before he goes and again when he gets back, but, in between, his ship is his world and he is the master.

This book is not just for ideal sailing wives—it is for all four categories and for wives and girl friends being introduced to this wide and complex subject for the first time.

The men, being enthusiasts, accept all sorts of hardships cheerfully, while we, not even liking the idea much at this stage, tend to see the discomforts and inconveniences first and, with luck, learn to see the pleasures in due course. Men either thrust us into the whole business too forcefully or sit us in a corner of the cockpit and expect us to enjoy ourselves. The galley is handed to us on a plate, and feelings are hurt if we show lukewarm enthusiasm for trying to cook under difficult conditions.

The doubtful pleasures

Many of us had not so much as thought about yachting before we met our husbands, or boy friends, and if we admit it honestly our interest was not sparked by enthusiasm so much as an effort to please and impress. We soon find it's not all plain sailing.

Often it is this first introduction to sailing that affects a woman's attitude to the sea. Either it appeals to her at once or she must learn about it and accept its challenge. The sea is never the same for more than an hour or two at a time. Winds change, tides turn, skies alter, night follows day, and throughout there is the boat to sail and she demands constant attention. If there are bad times they don't last for long; nor, unfortunately, do the good times. Even ardent enthusiasts swear never to go to sea again after a particularly tough sail. They are never ashore for more than a day, however, before they are planning their next trip.

What we must try to understand is what sailing means to a man. In his workaday job he is often routine-bound; he may have a dozen bosses and not much responsibility really, and no man worth being called male enjoys this. His boat offers challenge, responsibility and a chance to be the absolute master. Moreover, the problems he faces at sea are real ones and not paper tigers. His mistakes come home with a vengeance. His triumphs are full of flavor. In fact at sea modern, urbanized, office-bound man becomes a male in his real element.

A woman's place

Take a look round at women sailors who have tackled ocean crossings or distinguished themselves as cruising yachtswomen in home waters, and it's obvious that if she puts her mind to it a woman can do just as good a job as a man. That is not quite what this book is about. There can be only one skipper aboard the family cruiser. It is the woman/mate who is content to leave the command in male hands, but who would like to do a better job, for whom this book is written.

This young family believes in starting the children young and starting them right

The demands upon brute strength made by small modern yachts are few. Many elderly men or those not so strong physically have less beef than women, but the illusion of "man's work" persists and we are content to flatter the male ego. Where a woman comes into her own is in the small details of seagoing.

A knowledgeable woman on board a short-handed sailboat is as great a safety factor as a set of lifejackets aboard a boat in which the skipper has to do everything himself while lacking the wide experience of a single-handed sailor. If in an emergency a woman can take over the helm while he goes forward to struggle with sails, if she can start the engine, plot a position on the chart, or handle the anchor, she halves his labor. If she can take a night watch alone so that he can get some badly needed rest, she doubles his chances of remaining properly in control should an emergency arise later. Of course, the more rest he is able to get the better he can join in and enjoy trips ashore once the passage is over.

Some women tend to be shy of appearing nautical know-it-alls; some take the opposite line and regard those select few ocean-racing women as awesome beings never to be emulated. This, incidentally, is often far from the truth. Ocean racing is almost exclusively a male game and of those women who race, very, very few have the chance to handle sails or take an active part in the running of the ship at sea. Their place is in the galley and they are content to leave it that way. Cooking during a race is often a gruelling and gruesome business and women who tackle it—I speak from experience—have a full-time job. By the same token, the small-sailboat wife may not be such a specialist, but she is usually a more knowledgeable seawoman since she has a hand in every part of the operation. More often than not the offshore-racing wife remains ignorant of the arts and joys of seamanship.

Panics and alarms

Despite newspaper accounts of yachting tragedies, the dangers of sailing are surprisingly slight—far, far less than those of

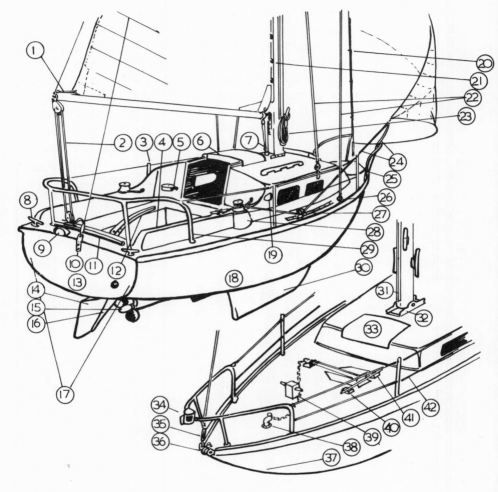

Fig. 1: Parts of a Boat
1. Mainsail clew outhaul
2. Mainsheet
3. Stanchions
4. Cockpit coaming
5. Steering compass
6. Sliding hatch
7. Mainsail tack downhaul
8. Mooring cleat
9. Stern light
10. Backstay chainplate
11. Mainsheet traveler or horse

12. Tiller
13. Transom
14. Rudder blade
15. Propeller
16. Rudder skeg
17. Quarters
18. Bilge
19. Sidelight
20. Jib hanks
21. Mainsail slides
22. Shrouds
23. Main halyard coil

24. Jib sheets
25. Bow pulpit
26. Turnbuckle
27. Sliding fairlead
28. Winch pedestal
29. Stern pulpit
30. Bilge keel
31. Mast foot
32. Mast step
33. Fore hatch
34. Combination sidelights
35. Forestay turnbuckle

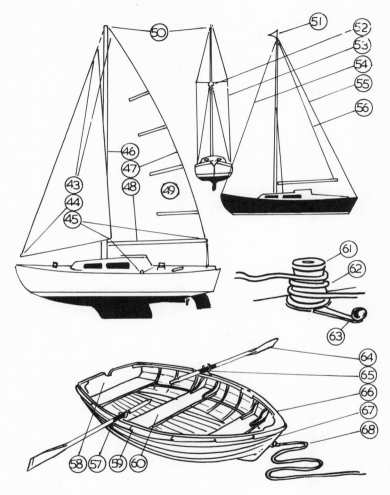

36. Stem roller fairlead
37. Stem
38. Chain navel pipe
39. Samson post
40. Anchor chocks
41. Danforth-type anchor
42. Lifelines
43. Head of sail
44. Tack of sail
45. Clew of sail
46. Mainsail luff
47. Mainsail leech

48. Foot of mainsail
49. Sail battens
50. Mastheads
51. Burgee
52. Hounds and spreaders
53. Topmast shroud
54. Forestay
55. Backstay
56. Topping lift
57. Oar leather
58. Transom
59. Bumper

60. Thwart
61. Sheet winch (bottom action)
62. Turns
63. Winch handle
64. Oar blade
65. Oarlock
66. Gunwale
67. Stem
68. Painter

motoring. In 90 percent of all mishaps the trouble is caused by over-cockiness, unsuitable boats or gear, lack of knowledge, or seasickness. A small sailboat need not get into serious trouble even though her crew are beginners, so long as they don't attempt too much, and learn all they can all the time.

A typical gentle cruise at sea in a small family yacht is not too ambitious at first—or shouldn't be. With a two-weeks' holiday ahead a yacht might spend perhaps five or six days at sea and possibly make one night passage. The rest of the time will be spent puttering about or ashore sightseeing, or swimming on some sandy beach. Of the total time there will probably be one or two days when the going is hard, wet and tough; but providing the crew have not set themselves an impossible itinerary and there is no need for a back-at-all-costs return passage, there is no reason why the yacht should ever be at sea in bad weather. She day-hops

His boat offers challenge and responsibility, but above all it gives him a chance to get away from workaday routine

from port to port or maybe makes the odd day-night-day passage if the weather is very settled. If bad weather threatens, she holes up somewhere—if it is possible to do so safely—her crew knowing full well that she need not be driven to sea due to shortage of time. At all costs it is the safety of the ship and crew that matters most, not how far she can go in the time or how brilliantly the skipper may prove himself in a gale. Hard weather experience should come by degrees.

The pros and cons of passage-making in bad weather don't come within the scope of this book. However, the main points are mentioned because whether the men realize it or not, it is usually the women on board who make the decisions.

Humoring them

Men in charge of boats, as I have indicated earlier, nearly always

The sea wife who takes an active part in handling the ship soon finds herself bitten by the sailing bug

change character. Even the meekest mouse ashore has been known to thunder out orders in his character of deep-sea mariner. Only *we* know how phony it is at times. Men are only as good as their knowledge of the sea allows them to be. Their decisions, if they should turn out wrong, mean a loss of face which is often covered up with a cloak of expertise. "Ah well, yes," they'll say, "I know we missed the tide, couldn't find the buoy and had to spend all night out, but then I'd reckoned on that trough of low pressure filling in and giving us a fair nor'westerly so that . . ." and so on.

The point of all this is that a woman who lacks diplomacy and nags a man about his mistakes forces him to weigh every decision he makes in terms of whether he can face up to her censure if he should be wrong. Thus he can never weigh up a situation in terms of technicality alone. He is concerned with the emotional situation first and the safety of the boat second.

What happens, for instance, if he decides to make for shelter rather than press on, and instead of the day becoming nasty it turns out sunny and warm with a gentle breeze? Do you say, "There you are, I told you so, I knew it would be all right?" Think twice. Another day, for the sake of peace, he may go against his better judgment and this time the weather forecast may be right. You could get a scolding.

There can be only one person on board to make the decisions. Wives should not undermine their skipper's authority, but they should help to influence him to do the right and safe thing at all times. Whether we like it or not, in the end it's usually the wife who is at the root of major decisions—no matter who gives the orders! Men often like to discuss a problem, outlining the arguments for and against, more for the sake of reviewing the situation aloud than for any expected contribution from their wives. Obviously a "Yes dear, No dear," response is as unhelpful as it is vapid; but an intelligent interest *is* helpful, and just occasionally a woman can, albeit innocently, put her finger on the very point of the matter. Joke or not, women are intuitive, so let intuition play its part by all means. It could well be that a wife's guileless contribution provides the answer to the whole problem, in which case her husband will think it was his idea all along. Let him.

Seasickness—the bogey

To most of us seasickness is the prime bogey of all. A lot of us feel seasick, but many live in dread of being sick whether they are or not. On short coastal passages where there isn't much need to go below, sickness is rare. The yacht is at sea for perhaps six or eight hours; such meals as may be needed are usually of the packed lunch variety prepared before sailing, so the most that is needed is a hot drink or two under way. Providing the cook doesn't try to stay below to cook a full meal the odds are that seasickness won't occur at all.

There is a lot one can do to overcome the bugbear of seasickness when a longer passage is envisaged. A fat-free, well-balanced diet for a few days before sailing helps, and it is a good idea to start taking anti-sickness pills in plenty of time before a passage—say a couple of days in advance. Make certain all the crew have a good hot meal (not too heavy) before sailing and that the first two or three meals are prepared in advance. Plenty of sandwiches, pies, soups, and stews can be prepared and the latter kept hot in thermos jugs. This means there is no need to spend time below preparing food during the first vital hours when the stomach is settling down to the motion of the boat.

Pills make some people sleepy, others thirsty, so try different makes until you find the one which suits you best. (*See also* Chapters 12 and 14.) Keep warm, keep busy, and wear a safety harness on deck if feeling at all dopey. If below, lie down at once unless you are busy with chores, in which case do them as quickly as possible and get plenty of air. Keep liquids to a minimum but don't become dehydrated. Have a few sweets, such as peppermints, handy in case a mouth freshener is needed and fairly dry crackers to tempt appetites which balk at everything else. In many cases seasickness goes after a few hours, leaving ravenous appetites to cope with all the pre-packed food, thus giving the cook breathing space to collect herself before preparing the next meal.

In extreme cases seasickness may mean that crew efficiency is reduced to a point which is dangerous to the efficiency of the ship. Never be ashamed to admit to seasickness, or to make for port if everybody is feeling weak. Initially general queasiness is no reason for giving up, but if after twenty-four to thirty hours at sea everybody is becoming weakened it is wise to consider doing so for a while. This doesn't mean making a blind dash for any shelter as there may be dangers in doing so. A woman's counsel of advice often takes over at this stage. Men may be willing to risk a dash for port solely to relieve their unhappy wives. Don't let them.

2/Wives and Boat Buying

A woman, totally inexperienced though she may be, starts to use her influence at the earliest of all stages—the actual buying of the boat. Nowadays, yacht builders are beginning to realize that the woman's influence in the choice of a boat is something which must be considered seriously.

Once upon a time when a man wanted a yacht, he either bought secondhand or went to a designer with fixed ideas about the sort of boat he wanted. Then the builder went to work on the design and the result, with a few compromises, was his chosen boat. Not any more. The majority of buyers of small sailboats have a less well-defined idea of what they want. The choice or the market is large, most of the craft of a similar size and type offering much the same features and performance.

Choosing a boat

Assuming that a husband and wife want, say four berths, seagoing ability, reasonable speed, fiber glass construction, twin keels, and so on—all within a price bracket—then the interior layout, the galley arrangements, the lighting, the upholstery and even the curtains can tip the balance. Usually the husband is so delighted that his wife is interested in buying the boat that he gladly overlooks one or two features which he may not like about the boat in order to let her have her way.

However, the wife should not be too easily influenced by the below-deck trimmings. First and foremost it is the performance of the boat that matters. While an out-and-out miniature ocean racer may be wrong for family seagoing, the big, boxy, floating caravan is far from ideal either. The woman who is going to have any say in choosing a boat should prime herself with a few facts

13

by reading some books and then by comparing the sales literature in the light of what she has learned. If this is beyond her scope, she should at least keep an eye lifted to the features of the boats considered and be prepared to yield a point or two. For instance, although a spacious galley may look good and be ideal on a river cruiser, a smaller galley in which it is possible for the cook to wedge herself securely is a much better bet in a seagoing cruiser.

Broadly speaking, the rather tubby little sailboat with palatial headroom and accommodation usually has too much boat above water to make her a good boat sailing to windward—against a head wind and sea, in fact. She may be buoyant and safe, but without her engine to help her she may not get along very fast when conditions are against her. At the other extreme, the longer, slimmer, deeper yacht, with less windage from a lower cabin top and so forth, is usually a powerful seagoer that can be threshed to windward in a strong wind and sea—and very wet it is too. Somewhere between the two is the happy average, and this may mean sacrificing a bit of head-room or having a cramped toilet compartment.

The family sailboat to accommodate two adults and two children may have her bunks so arranged that the children can be tucked in the fo'c'sle leaving the saloon for the grown-ups, who stay up later and may want to entertain friends. Ideally the toilet should be accessible from the saloon. The boat should have a good, big cockpit with sensible life rails round it as well as round the whole deck.

Many families have found their ideal in a sailing catamaran or trimaran. These are usually of modest sail area so that the old fear of capsize (since they have no deep ballast keel to self-right them) becomes very remote. The arrangement of berths in each of the two or three hulls makes it possible to bed the children down quite separately, and the fact that there is very little angle of heel when sailing makes life aboard much simpler and more comfortable. The pros and cons of whether to choose a conventional boat or a multihull type, whether to go for ballast keel or twin keels, and so forth, don't come within the scope of

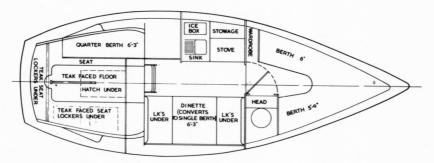

Fig. 2: The *Westerly Cirrus,* a typical 22-foot sailboat. She sleeps four and her accommodation layout is particularly suitable for the small family

This deck view of a cruising catamaran shows the amount of living space in the main cabin and the area of deck space. The two hulls have bunks, galley, toilet, etc.

this book, but they are mentioned briefly in passing to give the sailing wife some idea of the considerations to be made and to encourage her to take an interest in all aspects of the boat, quite apart from her immediate interest in the accommodation.

Choosing the extras

The boat once bought, a sailing wife comes into her domestic own at once. In all probability the basic below-deck equipment will be fitted: cooker, toilet, sink, water pump, bunk mattresses, cushions, dish stowage, etc. But the rest—pots and pans, dishes, sleeping bags, and so on—is up to the owner, or to be more precise, the owner's wife.

The wise sea wife goes for the most modern and up-to-date equipment available and does not make do with old, battered semi-worn pans and blankets in the mistaken idea that anything will do afloat. A new boat will most likely have spongeable bunk covers. If you are buying secondhand and they are not fitted, it is worth considering having mattresses and cushions re-covered in this type of material. Settee cushions in particular have to stand up to hard wear, and to dampness, and as they have to be used for sleeping at night, it is essential to be able to get them dry.

So far as cooking and dish washing are concerned, good quality non-stick pans are worth their weight in gold. There is always a shortage of water, particularly when it comes to washing dishes, so pans that wipe clean should be the first priority in any galley. There is the added advantage that food can be practically dry-fried in non-stick frying pans, and with a minimum of fat to clean up the major parts of the dish washing can be accomplished with paper towels (which can be used for wiping the dishes and cutlery, too) in readiness for the final rinse in fresh water.

When it comes to dishes the latest, break-resistant materials such as melamine are ideal, just as cutlery made of stainless steel takes a lot of beating since there is no danger of its rusting. Choose for preference deep dish plates which will hold good helpings of soup and stew, and good deep fruit dishes also. Take the trouble to get plastic glasses; they are well worth the extra cost.

Many small sailboats still use blankets as bunk warmers, but there is no doubt at all that sleeping bags, particularly those filled and covered with nylon or Dacron, beat them hands down when it comes to convenience and warmth. They stow easily and do away with the need for three or more blankets. Also they dry rapidly if they get damp. Another point is that blankets make fluff—a lot of fluff in a confined space. Cushions need careful choice and again it's worth going for Dacron-filled or foam rubber types which dry more quickly if they get wet.

It is useful to have some stout plastic bags for stowing items like sleeping bags and cushions when they are not required, particularly if the boat is left for any length of time. This way they will stay dry right through the season.

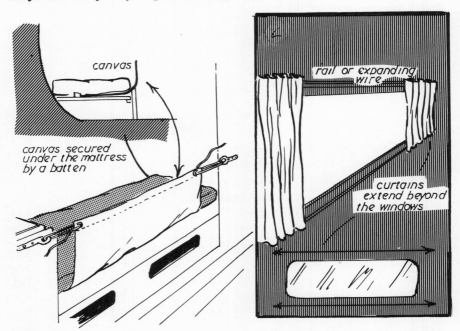

Fig. 3: Unless a bunk has side screens or "bunkboards" it is impossible to sleep in it when the ship is heeled and it is uphill. Simple screens as shown are adequate and make a useful safe spot for putting things even when day sailing. The strings, or lanyards, serve to tighten the top edge

Fig. 4: Curtains are essential for privacy when lying alongside a quay. See that they extend beyond the windows, otherwise it won't be possible to pull them right back when light is needed

Not items to buy necessarily, but vital if the crew are to sleep easily in a seaway, are bunk boards of some sort. If none are fitted, consider having some canvas or wooden bunk boards made up (Fig. 3).

Added refinements, but essential if the boat is to be used by people outside the immediate family, are linings for sleeping bags. Again modern materials are best and there are already linings available in brushed nylon and Dacron, but they are simple to make up in any material.

Since a large proportion of sailing time is spent in harbor, berthed alongside or among other yachts on moorings or at anchor, curtains of some sort are essential. Modern yachts are light and airy below, which means good big ports or windows, and a decided lack of privacy. The best arrangement is to have curtains—and probably for long wear plastic material is the most suitable—which fit close against the ports (Fig. 4).

Some families find their ideal in a powerboat. Although they are not faced with the problems of wind and sails, power cruising enthusiasts still have to cope with tides, navigation, handling, anchoring, and so on

Lighting is important. If electric light is not fitted the alternatives are either oil or dry battery lanterns or pressure stoves in either gas or kerosine. Pressure lamps give out the best illumination. Care and attention to safe stowage is important and a reflector must be fitted above lamps if they are suspended under the deckhead.

When it comes to basins, dust pans, trays and other small items of equipment, again it is worth choosing plastic. This applies to galley storage containers as well and you can't have too many of these. Remember perishables must be sealed against damp sea air and in containers which won't rust. Incidentally, a plastic dinghy bailer makes an excellent dust pan. It's smaller and more compact than the normal domestic variety and it serves a double purpose since it can be used for bailing out the dinghy tender

An ideal accommodation layout for family sailing. This one has a separate forward cabin for the smaller members of the family, as well as separate toilet to port and hanging locker to starboard. Here the dinette has been converted to a double bunk, so she will sleep five

too. Choose a good stout plastic milk container, preferably one with a pourer, and don't forget the small vital extras like can opener, bread board, strainer, mop, scourer, etc., to mention but a few.

Does the type of sailing you have in mind warrant a pressure cooker and/or an ice box? In both cases I would say, sail for a season without them, only time will tell whether they will earn

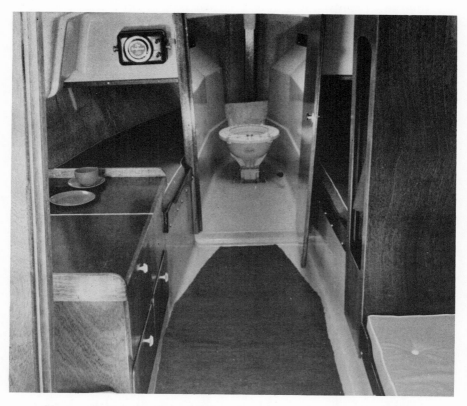

Many sailboats, such as this one, have an open plan accommodation. The forward bunks run in tunnels alongside the toilet, which is in a separate compartment. Some privacy is given by the hanging cupboard to starboard and the cooking cabinet to port

their keep. Personally I have sailed for years without either. What I do consider important on a small boat is a grill pan; if the stove doesn't include a grill, consider one of the cylindrical diffuser grills or flat toasters which fit on a top burner. They don't grill, of course, but they make good toast and widen the scope of meals considerably.

Two other small items which have always rated top priority with me are the asbestos mat and the rubber mat; the former because it's practically impossible to turn bottled gas down low enough to simmer without it blowing out, and the rubber mat on which to stand hot pans taken straight from the stove. The cook afloat becomes something of a juggler, more often than not coping with three or more pans on a two-burner stove, and she must have somewhere to put the hot pans safely. The rubber mat has the added advantage that it is comparatively non-slip and keeps the pans fairly well anchored, too.

Finally, not an item of galley equipment, but something which should be included aboard every sailboat, large or small, a well-stocked first aid kit. (*See* Chapter 14 for a list of what it should contain.)

When you have settled on the equipment, ideally there should be ample locker or storage space for stowing it and all the ship's stores as well as all the personal gear required when sailing. If there isn't, manage as best you can during the first trip or two until it becomes apparent just how much extra stowage is needed, and where it is needed. Fitting extra lockers into wooden hulls is a simple enough matter, but fiber glass boats sometimes present problems.

Now is the time to enlist the owner's help; let him tackle the problem as best he can and reach a happy compromise between the amount of storage space you *could* use and the actual amount which it is possible to fit into so small a space. With a bit of forethought and planning it is amazing how much "essential" gear can be weeded out. To start with, leave ashore next time any personal gear not used during the previous trip. Be honest: if you manage without it once it can't be so essential, can it?

3/Living in a Confined Space

Despite the fact that the idea of owning a seagoing yacht is to go to sea, the greater part of all time spent aboard it is, as I have mentioned, at anchor or berthed alongside. At sea, there are usually some of the ship's company down below resting or else they are in the cockpit enjoying the sailing. In harbor, the center of activity is often down below and what seemed to be a spacious cabin suddenly becomes a mass of arms and legs and people moving around getting in each other's way. It is a fact that a cabin full of landsmen seems twice as full as it should. Boat-people develop a knack of occupying a small space which makes it seem larger than it is. The way they move and when they move is all part of this knack and it is worth looking at in detail.

First and foremost, the cook has supreme rights when she is preparing a meal. There must be no shoving past her when she is at the stove; if the children want to go on deck they must use the forehatch, and so on. This is fair and it is sense—if nobody is to be scalded and the cook is to stay sane. It is her right and she should demand it. The wise skipper will busy himself on deck if the sailboat is very small and cramped or he will study his charts for the leg on the next day. Children can be similarly occupied.

The same applies, of course, when serious navigation is in progress. The navigator expects to get supreme rights when he is at his chart table and this is one time when, if she is wise, the cook will keep away from her stove, since on most small sailboats the chart table doubles as putting-down space for the galley.

Really, living in a small space all boils down to tidiness and cooperation. Life on board with two, three or maybe even four people eating, sleeping, washing, and all the rest of it, in a space probably no larger than the kitchen of a bachelor's apartment, can be chaos and misery; on the other hand it can just as easily be fun, for all that it is decidedly cramped fun.

Stowage space is the first bugbear and I have yet to find a sailboat with enough of it to take all the gear brought on board, mainly because the more lockers there are the more gear each

When the dinette is converted this boat sleeps five. There isn't room to sleep all the people shown, but there is plenty of sitting-down space when it comes to entertaining

person brings along in the hope that it will go in somewhere. Wise owners decide on the amount of personal gear the crew should bring with them; this certainly happens in the ocean racing fleet where weight, probably more than space, is the overriding factor.

This is where sensible planning of personal gear and of ship's stores pays off. Ideally there should be one locker for each person for personal gear and a hanging locker which is shared by all, as is the space for oilskins, etc. Any locker space not taken up by ship's stores can then be divided again.

The idea of a place for everything and everything in its place, with cooperation from every member of the crew, works well during the day when life is orderly and much of the time is spent on deck, but what happens at night is another matter. Four people sitting up and moving around take up much less space than four people lying down, and it is at night, and particularly first thing in the morning when the ship begins to come to life again, that a well-organized routine is needed. If there are children on board the business of turning in is divided in two with the children bedding down first, thus easing congestion. If the crew is made

This view of the companionway and part of the cabin shows how neat stowage of dishes, sheetbags, and the like helps to give an uncluttered appearance. The navigator's table slides out of the way when not in use

up entirely of adults the only sensible arrangement is to go to
bed by numbers, leaving the last one up to extinguish lights, check

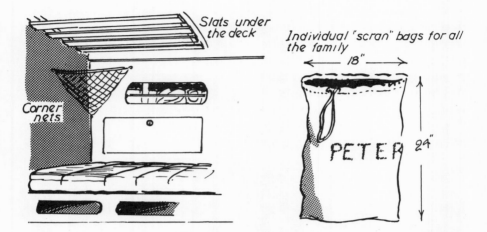

Fig. 5: Bags of different shapes and sizes (a typical one is illustrated
here) are useful on board. There are other ways of improving stowage space. A slatted rack under the deckhead takes charts, maga-
zines, etc., and a corner net is handy for clothes when the bunk is
in use

that gas is turned off, that the anchor light is all right, and do
all the last-minute jobs.

On a sailing trip there is more to turning in at night than this.
The ship is away from her home port, she is "on passage," and
to all intents and purposes she should be ready to go to sea at
any time. It just might be necessary to get under way again in
a matter of five minutes. Could it be done? On a well-organized
ship anything is possible, and providing all the gear not in use
is safely stowed away in the correct lockers so that each member
of the crew can quickly find what he wants, there should be no
difficulty at all. You never know, a worsening weather forecast,
a change of wind direction, might make it imperative to get to

sea in moments, so the aim of any crew, at any time, should be to be fit and ready for sea in five minutes.

I have always found it a good idea to have a few bags which can be used to take oddments of gear at night. These can be hung from hooks, or pushed into corners and then rolled up out of the way during the day when not needed. Make or buy them in various shapes and sizes for easier stowing, and in a good strong material like canvas, and allow at least one for each member of the crew. These will certainly save fumbling and rummaging around if it should be necessary to get under way during the night (Fig. 5).

To me the worst time of all is early in the morning. Four bodies bumbling and barging around, sleeping bags and gear everywhere, everyone trying to wash and dress at once; youngsters calling for breakfast; father watching the weather, trying to listen to the forecast, consulting tides and coming out with the popular statement, "We should be over the bar by 7:30" (and it's now 7:25!) —no, you would have to be a saint to enjoy a morning like this.

Again I've found the only workable solution to the problem is to get up and dress by numbers. Preferably starting with father, who has to look after the riding light, etc. If he's well trained he gets the water going for coffee or tea and washing. Then the rest follow with mother last, if she has any choice, drinking her coffee or tea in peace and combining her own getting up with stowing away sleeping bags and a general quick clean-up before preparing breakfast. By this time the working party on deck has everything shipshape and a well-organized crew sit down to a well-organized breakfast. The less said about rainy mornings the better, but usually a well-organized crew will take such a novelty in its stride, and father possibly will not object to parading on deck in oilskins and sou'wester while the ship is readied for inspection below.

So, fundamentally, living in a confined space afloat is very much like living in a tent or small caravan, as anyone who has had to up-tent and move in seconds as floodwaters rise will confirm.

4/On the Domestic Side

Just as the ship's gear will only stand up to the rigor and strain of hard weather if it is looked after, so will the crew only keep going at their peak if they are well looked after. It is the sea wife's job to see that the crew are well fed on board and that when the opportunity for rest comes they can sleep undisturbed.

Apart from the effects of seasickness, fatigue is more often than not due to insufficient sleep, or inability to sleep. When cruising there is a great deal the sea wife can do to keep the vessel orderly and reasonably quiet below to give those trying to sleep a fair chance of catching up on much needed rest. All equipment and gear should be stowed safely so that it doesn't toss around as the ship heels or lurches, and annoying rattles and squeaks should be silenced. In addition the cook should plan her catering to ensure that she has no need to delve into the bilge or forage in lockers, especially at night.

As well as sleep, regular feeding is vital; food gives the body not only energy, but warmth, too. It's all the more unfortunate that just as the going gets rougher and the crew is subjected to periods of intense endeavor, the preparation of food becomes more and more difficult and the temptation to leave it until conditions improve is great. This is fatal. Obviously conditions will improve eventually, but in all probability long before that the lack of food will begin to have its effect. Gradually the crew feel exhausted, cold, hungry and tired, and their efficiency deteriorates considerably. Sickness may take over and already it may be too late to stoke up the body heat and energy again.

At this time beware of alcoholic drinks. That alcohol is an excellent medicine for those who are wet, cold, and exhausted is well known; not so well known is the fact that this applies only if they can rest and keep warm. In fact, in the old days of sailing ships a drink all round was given to any of the crew who had to make intensive efforts, such as reefing sails in a bad gale. But, and it is a big but, only if they were going below to keep warm.

The pick-you-up—rum, whiskey, what have you—gives a quick deep glow of warmth which stays there to comfort the body so

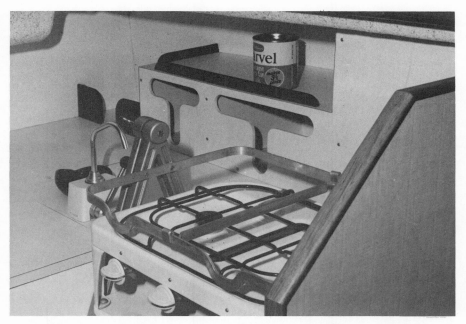

Two-burner bottled gas stove with gimbals. Note the fiddles round the stove also and the neat lockers for plates

long as it is warm, but on deck in cold, wet conditions the effect quickly wears off leaving the crew disappointed at the sudden let-down; and they are weaker and colder than before. This being so, a good many owners keep alcohol tucked away for emergency only or for when the ship is safely at rest after a hard passage.

During a passage, food of some sort—chocolate, nuts, crackers, cheese, fruit, and cold drinks—must be available if producing anything more complicated is out of the question. In fact what is wanted is a selection of high protein food to help replenish waning energy.

This, of course, is looking on the blackest side and assuming that the cook has not prepared a meal (hot drinks, soup etc.) in readiness for such conditions. An unusual state of affairs but worth considering because, inevitably, be it sooner or later, the unexpected does happen. What starts off as a gentle afternoon sail can become an all-night vigil—such are the delights of sailing. However, the ship's cook who has thought about her tasks will not be caught napping. Ideally she will never let her ship go to sea for an afternoon sail, a day hop, or an overnight sortie without enough spare food on board to keep the crew going for twenty-four hours if the need should arise.

Planning below

In point of fact the times are very, very few when cooking of some sort is impossible. The well-planned galley with equipment and

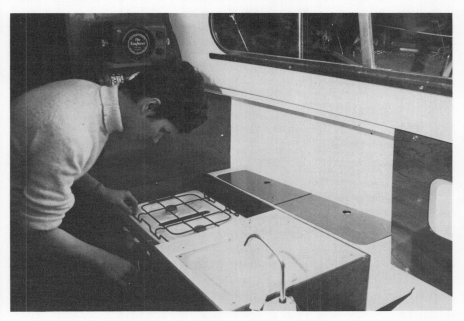

A small sailboat's galley. The stove is fixed but can be fitted with fiddles to hold pans secure. There is plenty of locker space under the cooker and sink and good deep lockers behind. A special top that fits over the whole galley gives extra putting-down space

stores handily stowed, and the stove well gimballed, eases the cook's problems enormously. I always find a few minutes looking around the galley on other sailboats well worthwhile. Designers and interior planners have come up with some excellent and novel ideas for stowage, lockers, work tables, sinks and cooking compartments, and the modern small sailboat is a very workmanlike and practical proposition. Whether we own a modern sailboat or an old craft with accommodation planned in a more traditional style, it is always worth keeping an eye open for new ideas in galley equipment and stowage, and improvements, however small, which make the galley cook's life run more smoothly.

Is the mug stowage the best possible arrangement? Do they stack neatly or are they liable to come skimming off their hooks in a bumpy sea (Fig. 6)? If it is not possible to stow plates and dishes quickly without juggling them there is obviously something wrong. It should be possible to get food out of lockers on either tack without everything cascading out. If it isn't, consider a strip of expanding curtain wire across the inside of the locker front to hold the contents in.

A quiet ship below is something to aim for. Always have some foam rubber handy to wedge against plates, dishes, tins, pans, etc., which clatter and bang as the ship moves. The grill pan is another great disturber of the peace. Work out some system of keeping it securely anchored under way. Your own pet bugbear may not be the grill pan, but the kettle, bread board or tray. Whatever it is, find some solution and see what a difference it makes. If there is no sink on board which can be used for standing mugs in for filling when there is danger of spilling, invest in a deep plastic box or tray or dish pan that will serve the same purpose. Incidentally, on the subject of mugs, it is a sensible idea to have some specially deep ones for use in the cockpit when the going is rough.

Putting-down space in the galley is usually at a premium. If it really is short, consider a pull-out or folding flap table (Fig. 7). Neither need take up much room when not in use, but they could provide just the extra space needed at serving time.

Make certain that locker space is used to the best advantage. If lockers are very deep, try a divider across them—the back portion can be kept for lesser used items—or consider an extra shelf in high lockers.

If the cook is not already provided with a seat or rail to support herself without using her hands, see if it is possible to include a handhold above the stove and battens on the floor to give a firm foothold. They are very worthwhile additions even on a weekend sailboat (Fig. 8). A belt with which she can tie herself in so that both hands are free is another idea, especially if more ambitious trips are planned (Fig. 9).

It is usually possible to arrange for a good current of air below so that the cook can tackle her jobs in comfort. However, just occasionally the boat lies to the tide with the wind right aft and if the stove is situated in the companionway, the draft can become a problem. When this happens, consult the owner; a temporary

Fig. 6: Mugs stowed on hooks must not swing off as the ship heels over. A box with a slot for handles is one good stowage, or wooden blocks, one for each mug, can be screwed down

Fig. 7: A sliding table under the cooker is sometimes possible and very useful if the galley is small and putting-down space is limited

windbreak is not difficult to fix up or perhaps a riding sail can be set aft to help keep the boat head to wind.

A tent for harbor cooking and living is also a good idea. Fitted over the boom it effectively shuts in the cockpit and doubles the accommodation. It also helps the cook enormously in wet and windy weather, keeps rain from getting below and gives good privacy as well (Fig. 10). The tent need not cut down light below; it can be made from cloudy plastic, Dacron or thin canvas—the latter two fitted with flexible plastic windows.

Other main do's and don'ts concern seacocks to the head and the sink, but, of course, these apply to everyone on board, not just the sea wife. All seacocks are turned off between each cruise; some owners turn the toilet seacock off each time it is used, others never when the ship is being lived in. Really it depends on the type of toilet. If the top of the toilet bowl is below the waterline, seacocks should be shut off when the boat is left with no one

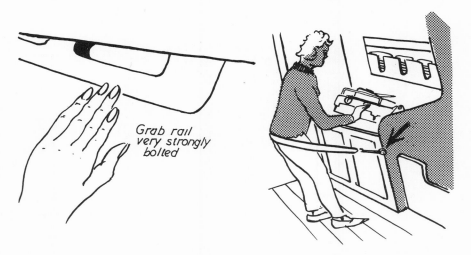

Grab rail very strongly bolted

Fig. 8: Rough weather bumps and bruises can be avoided if strong grab rails are provided below deck. Certainly the cook will find a rail like this helpful in a seaway

Fig. 9: Better still is a belt arrangement which gives the cook both hands free. This must be strong enough to take all her weight when the ship heels

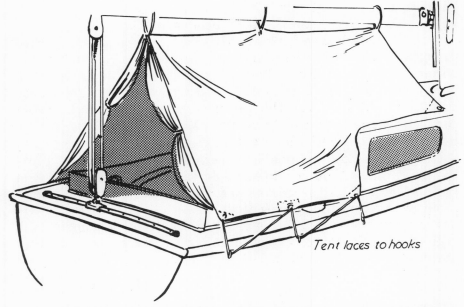

Tent laces to hooks

Fig. 10: A cockpit tent rigged when a small cruiser is at anchor can make all the difference, especially in wet weather. Any tentmaker or sailmaker will make one such as this

aboard; and if there is no vented loop on the discharge line, its cock should be closed when under sail. In most cases the sink seacock is turned off when the ship is sailing hard and always when she is left.

Water supplies are important, and if life on board is to go smoothly they must be used sensibly and with care. Half a gallon a person a day is the absolute minimum for drinking, tea- or coffee-making, etc.; this allows nothing for washing, cooking, and dish washing, so plan on at least two gallons for each person as the minimum. Don't be misled though by what you read about ocean-crossing yachtsmen and their water ration. You will probably be able to fill your water containers every day or so, so why deny yourself one of life's basic necessities?

About stoves

How is the stove fixed? Ideally for cooking in a seaway it should swing athwartships in gimbals—i.e. suspended so that its base doesn't come into contact with the side of the ship as it swings out, or project beyond the edge of its shelf as it swings towards the center (Fig. 11). If the stove should touch the side of the ship the sudden jerk as the swing is interrupted may be enough to throw pans off, and if it should swing too far in the other direction it may be knocked by the cook with the same result. On the other hand, in small sailboats of 18–24 feet, the cooker may be fixed but provided with rails or "fiddles" to keep pans from sliding off (Fig. 12). The assumption is that the very minimum of cooking will be done in conditions which merit a gimballed cooker. Hot

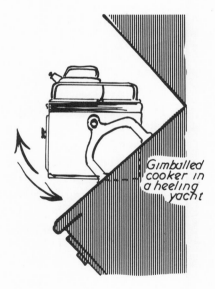

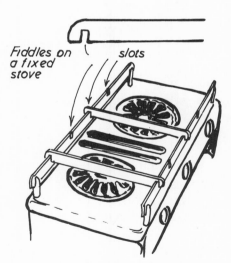

Fig. 11: A gimballed stove stays level no matter how steeply the yacht is heeling. Providing nothing stops the swing and no one jerks the stove the pans will stay secure

Fig. 12: A fixed stove can be fitted with adjustable fiddles (one type is illustrated). While fiddles hold a pan steady they cannot stop spillage from the pan itself

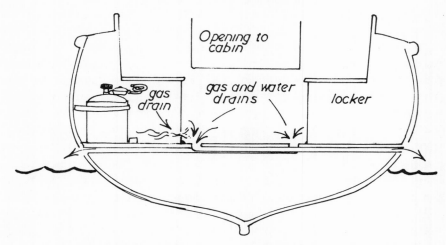

Fig. 13: Gas bottle stowage. The crossed drains to the cockpit ensure that water cannot run back into the cockpit when the boat is heeling. Some boats have the drains passing out through the stern instead. The gas bottle in its gas-tight locker has a drain hole which allows any gas leak to escape via the cockpit drain pipes, but other gas lockers may have independent drains which run straight out through the yacht's side

drinks, soup, and warming up of precooked stews, etc., can be coped with reasonably well in any but the worst conditions, or when life below is usually too hectic for cooking anyway. More often than not, only when at anchor or in port will the full-scale meal be attempted. A one-burner, portable, gimballed and bulkhead-mounted sterno stove (sometimes called a "swing stove") is a great boon in very rough weather.

Presumably the type of stove on board will depend on what was fitted originally in the case of a secondhand boat, or on the owner's choice in a new boat. It may be bottled gas; it may be kerosine. Both types have their followers, just as both have their drawbacks. With gas stoves there is a risk of explosion if, through carelessness, leaked gas has collected in the bilge. The kerosine stove, on the other hand, is inclined to be messy, smelly, and troublesome; however, it is safe.

The alcohol or kerosine stove takes longer to light and get going than the gas stove, which loads the score heavily in favor of the latter on the small sailboat where, more often than not, the stove is only needed for quick heat-ups for soups, stews, and fried snacks. One's personal choice and the type of sailing envisaged will decide which type of stove is chosen, but these points are worth bearing in mind. Obviously with use the problems of kerosine stoves can be ironed out, and the risk of explosion with gas stoves more or less eliminated if strict care is exercised.

If gas is the choice the gas cylinder itself should be stowed on deck if this is possible, or in a gas-tight cockpit locker with a drain (Fig. 13). This means that if there should be a leak of gas from the cylinder it is well clear of the bilges, so that any leaks below will be from the stove itself, and careful installation and maintenance at the joints precludes trouble there. The rest is up to the cook.

Here are the points to watch when using gas stoves afloat. The match must always be lighted before the gas taps are turned on; the flame should never be turned so low that it can blow out, allowing gas to escape; and careful watch must be kept on drafts in case they should blow the flame out. Never let pots and pans boil over—it could douse the flame. Between use always turn the gas off at the bottle, allowing any gas remaining in the pipes to burn out before turning the stove taps off. (And, incidentally, check each time that the taps are off before turning the bottle on again.) The habit of turning the gas off at the bottle each time is a safeguard against children fiddling with the knobs of the stove, as they are apt to do. Most cruisers with bottled gas stoves now carry a spare bottle and replacements are readily available at chandlers and boatyards.

With careful use galley stoves can have long, carefree lives. However, just in case of emergencies with them, or with any form of kerosine lamps, make sure there is a fire extinguisher handy to the galley, and make sure you know how to work it. The extinguisher should be placed so that it can be grabbed from the cockpit if need be. If this isn't possible, fit an additional extinguisher in the cockpit itself.

5/First Time Afloat

Strictly for beginners

In all probability the first time a woman goes out in a small yacht
she will be a passenger and nothing will be expected of her except
perhaps that she makes the coffee or tea. Passenger or not, first
impressions can be worrying in a strange setting, and in any case
no woman likes to look a complete fool.

The dinghy

It is possible to pick out the complete beginner before he or she
ever sets foot in a boat. In fact, how to set foot in a small boat
alongside a jetty, or steps, is the first thing to learn. Balance is
the essential. Usually the skipper will get in first and hold the
boat steady. The aim is to extend one leg towards the middle of
the dinghy floorboards while facing the jetty—in other words, to
step in backwards. This way you will have both hands on the
jetty keeping weight on them until ready to transfer it to the
feet. Once this is done, sit down where told to quickly and gently.
The odds are that the rower, helmsman or skipper, call him what
you like, will then push off and get moving. Sit amidships so that
the boat is on an even keel, unless he asks you otherwise.

Don't hold on to the sides; your fingers could get damaged when
the dinghy goes alongside the yacht. When she gets there you
may reach up and either hang on to the yacht's rail or fend her
off according to weather conditions. You will then, most probably,
be told to get aboard. This can be the tricky part. Get both hands
on the rail and transfer a knee to the deck first, then climb up
how you like. *Do not* push outwards at the dinghy with your feet
or try to step on one side of her. Keep your weight in the middle

all the time until you have transferred it to the yacht. Once aboard you may take the dinghy's painter or bow rope. When you have become experienced and if you are sitting in the bows of the dinghy, you will take the painter with you automatically because that's the bowman's job anyhow.

All of which is very elementary, perhaps, but also very important if you are not to look a fool.

The first sail

At this stage we must assume that the man in charge knows a bit about boats. If he happens to be a husband and a raw beginner he should be encouraged to go on a sailing course to learn the rudiments; if you both go, so much the better. Nowadays there are so many small craft afloat that it is very difficult to learn by trial and error completely from scratch without risk of collision. Looking on the graver side of things, it is rather presumptuous to tackle seagoing as a complete novice, because the sea makes no distinctions between professional and novice. One should know how to handle a boat with fair competence under power or sail; be able to tackle basic navigation; know the essentials of the Rules of the Road at sea (the maritime highway code); and understand the workings of the tides, the technique of anchoring, and so on.

Let us assume that the craft in question is a small sailboat with an auxiliary engine. She could as easily be a small power yacht, of course, and here may I digress? The belief that a motor boat is simple to handle for any motorist is a false one. She is easier to "drive" and one need not know the ways of wind and sails, but the basic seagoing knowledge of weather, tides, drift and so forth remains important and whether the boat is driven by motor or sail this basic homework must be done if the crew are to be safe at sea.

Getting under way is an operation which almost always involves a certain amount of tension. Unlike a car, a boat begins to move and continues to move from the moment her moorings

A newcomer may find this sort of sailing angle a bit frightening. Spray will be flying, things slipping and sliding around, and there will be chaos below if things have not been properly stowed. The motion always seems worse below, so this would not be the time to go to sort things out

are cast off. A car can be parked on the hand brake; not so a boat. She drifts on wind or tide, or both, she swings broadside, rocks and rolls and is altogether unmanageable until either the engine is started or the sails are set. Hence when getting under way there will be a few moments before she has gathered headway when she is virtually out of control. Without headway she cannot be steered.

More often than not a sailing yacht of any size, particularly in the hands of a comparative novice, gets under way under power and sets sail later when clear of her own and other moorings. If for some reason the engine should stop there may well be a good deal of panic, and the best place for a passenger is down below out of the way!

Once the sails are set and the engine is stopped a good deal of activity takes place. In a good breeze the yacht may heel over until she is virtually on her side, and this can seem alarming to a newcomer. However, small sailboats cannot capsize because of the ballast keel under them which acts as a counter-balance. Sailing dinghies can, and do, capsize, but then they are designed so that the weight of their crew forms the counter-balance and depending on how hard they are being sailed they may capsize if pushed too far. By the same token there is little likelihood of a sturdy, beamy dinghy capsizing unless she is being sailed daredevil fashion.

As the yacht leaves the shelter of her anchorage and meets the larger waves of the open sea, she will begin to pitch and corkscrew about, possibly hurling sheets of spray over her decks. Again this can seem alarming at first, but confidence in knowing that the boat and crew are familiar with these conditions should allow the passengers to begin to feel the joy of exhilarating conditions and the freedom of open waters.

At this stage a passenger is unwise to go below. Until she gets used to the motion it is risking seasickness to try, for instance, to make coffee or tea no matter how much she would like to make herself useful. Better to stay on deck and get the feel and the thrill of sailing. Should it prove to be a calm day with a gentle breeze and a more or less upright boat, well, of course, there is not much danger of seasickness and the newcomer can begin to get her sea legs below too.

Sooner or later a small yacht has to turn and make back for harbor, and if she has been battling against wind and wave on the way out she will be "running" on the way back. Suddenly the boat is upright, the wind seems to have dropped and the spray

On a run, things are more comfortable, usually. This boat, a *Westerly Nimrod,* is running before a moderate breeze and has her spinnaker set

stops breaking over the decks. The helmsman, who may have been full of chatter earlier, is likely to fall silent and appears to be concentrating hard. The fact is that in any sort of good breeze, running before the wind is often more difficult than the other points of sailing. The time may come when the boat must be "jibed" (see the following section on How a Boat Sails). The sail may come across with a heavy crash and she may heel far over before she recovers. Newcomers to sailing are apt to develop an early dread of jibing; often dating from a first-time trip and a sense that the yacht was somehow out of control. An accidental jibe can, in fact, be dangerous (hence the concentration of the helmsman), but no more so than a skid in a car, which can almost always be avoided with care and usually rectified by skill if it should happen due to unforeseen circumstances.

The final return to the mooring is the occasion of another spell of action by the crew. The stowing of sails, the starting of the engine, and the picking up of the buoy may all become tricky operations if wind and tide should render things difficult. The best place to be is below, out of the way, if a real scrimmage develops.

So much for that first sail. Most probably the passenger will have been given a few simple jobs to do, according to the weather, but the main thing is that she has had a chance to see, feel, and sense something of the small-boat game. There remains the return trip in the dinghy, and we have dealt with that problem. Suffice it so to say that if there is any sea running and the yacht is jumping about on her mooring, the transferring from yacht to dinghy must be done as quickly and smoothly as possible, remembering to step well into the middle of the dinghy and sit down as quickly as possible.

How a boat sails

It seems pointless to say more about the complexities of crewing until we have delved into the how and why of handling a boat under sail. Readers who are already knowledgeable on the subject

Some of the jobs a woman might well tackle on her first trips afloat. Helping to winch in the head-sails. Hanking on the jib. Stowing the main-sail

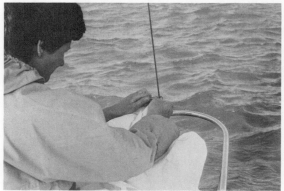

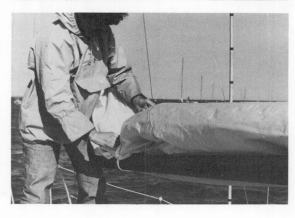

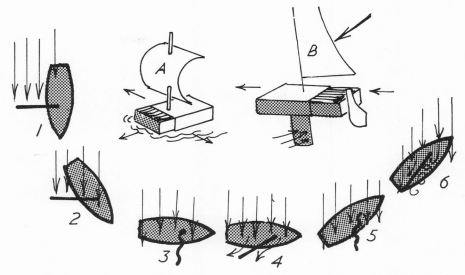

Fig. 14: How the wind drives a boat. The matchbox boat A can only sail downwind; she will go sideways if the wind blows from the other side. Boat B has a keel and a rudder to keep her straight. The keel stops her from being pushed sideways when the wind is on one side. Boats 1 to 6 show how a sail must be gradually trimmed in as a boat moves downwind and then across the wind and finally close hauled into the wind

might ignore this section. Those others who may have done quite a lot of sailing, but have not really understood the reasons for everything, may find a few answers here, and the complete beginner will find that a knowledge of the theory of sailing, is invaluable right from the start.

Anything can sail before the wind. A paper bag does so in style; the Portuguese man-of-war raises its jellyfish membrane and sails downwind happily; a yacht spreads wide her sails and, guided by her rudder, sails either dead before it, perhaps also setting her spinnaker, or she sails obliquely down-wind with the wind coming at her from one side of her stern or the other.

With the wind from one side, however, the picture begins to alter. A paper bag cannot sail *across* the wind because it would drift sideways and begin running again. A yacht would also drift sideways were it not for her keel which takes a grip upon the water. It is easier for her to go forward than sideways. If the sails were still fully out they would just flutter like flags, so they are trimmed in until they are full of wind, or asleep as the saying goes, and here comes the mystery of sails and wind. We could just leave matters by saying that they are "full" and forget the theory, but it has a bearing on efficient crewing later (Fig. 14).

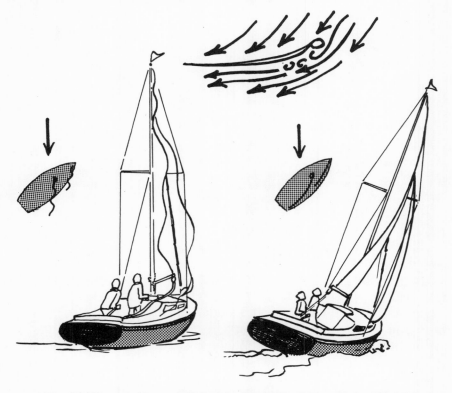

Fig. 15: The top diagram shows how wind currents pass either side of a close-hauled sail, eddying behind it and creating a low pressure "lift" area. An airplane wing acts in the same way except that it is driven forwards to create wind and the boat's "wing" is upright and the natural wind moves past it creating forward drive. The two yachts shown demonstrate a flapping sail which lacks drive and a correctly trimmed sail close hauled

Without becoming scientific, we can say that wind striking a sail from the side divides around it. Some is deflected along the front of the sail and the rest, eddying past it, flows round the back where it leaves a sort of dead area (rather like the back-eddy which forms behind a rock sticking up in the middle of a little stream). This dead area gives a sort of lift and contributes to the thrust of the sail against its mast. Just as the wing of an airplane lifts as the plane gathers speed and creates its own wind, so does wind blowing on and around a sail create "drive" (Fig. 15).

Now, if the sail is pulled in too flat at this stage it makes an unfavorable angle to the wind and although the boat will still move ahead, she heels over much more and gets far less drive from her sails. It is the constant adjustment of this angle of sail to wind which is the art of sail-trimming and good crewing. Once you are afloat and handling sails this theory will make sense to you.

A sailing craft cannot be made to sail dead into the wind. If she is pointed head to wind ("luffing up") her sails shake uselessly and she starts going backwards. Since she must get up wind

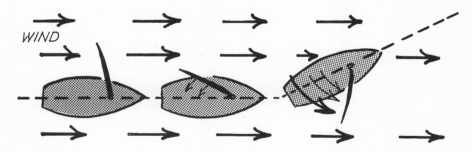

Fig. 16: A jibing sail is like a door which slams as the wind gets behind it. To jibe under control the boat is sailed straight while the sail is hauled in; she is then turned a little to bring the wind round to the other side of the sail and as it jibes the sheet is paid out smoothly around a cleat to reduce the shock. A jibe "all standing" from full out one side to full out the other can be safe if intended, but the sheet could catch someone round the neck, or the boom could catch the backstay when the jibe is uncontrolled

somehow she does the next best thing. Her sails are hardened in as tightly as possible (not strictly accurate, but no matter) and she is turned into the wind as far as she will go without their beginning to flutter. She is now close-hauled and will be lying at, let us say, 45 degrees to the wind.

Obviously, if her destination is a point dead to windward of her starting place she will not get there on this course, and so she zigzags, sailing with the wind first on one side of the sails and then on the other, turning head to wind each time she tacks or goes about. The theory of the airplane wing is illustrated very clearly when sailing close-hauled and tacking. The wind meets the sails, divides and deflects, increasing its own speed as it passes between the sails.

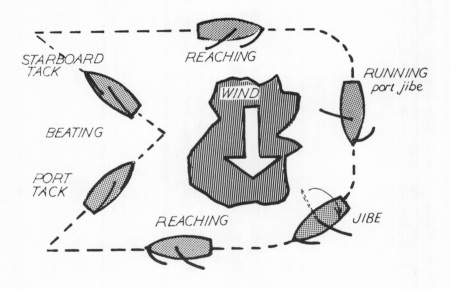

Fig. 17: Points of sailing. These are the main points, but many variants of them are used and sails are trimmed in or let out accordingly. The reaches shown are "broad" reaches, but there are close reaches (heading up a little bit more), and quartering reaches (wind a bit further aft). If the beating boat were pointed any closer to the wind than this she would be "pinching"

Back to running. We can now understand how a sailing boat sails across the wind or "reaches," how she tacks, and how she runs. Now for the theory of the dreaded jibe. We must imagine our boat running along with the wind dead behind her. Her mainsail can be regarded as a huge door, hinged to the mast and able to swing across the boat, while her jib is hinged to the forestay. Both are controlled at their "free" ends by means of sheets which are used to pull them in or let them out. Now, if our mainsail is fully let out so that it is stretching out over the water on one side of the boat, it is going to be held there by the pressure of the wind coming from astern. So long as the wind direction remains steady and the boat is steered straight nothing can go wrong, but should the wind shift out to one side so that it gets at the forward side of the sail, or should the helmsman let the boat curve off course so that the wind can get at that forward side, the whole thing can slam from one side of the boat to the other. A jibe, in fact (Fig. 16).

Between these three main points of sailing come the intermediate points: the quartering reach (wind on one side of the stern); the close reach (wind on the side and slightly ahead); and so on. It is only necessary to master the rudiments at this stage, but if they *are* mastered it will soon be evident even to the relative beginner when a sail needs trimming and it will be possible to anticipate things before they happen, too (Fig. 17).

The wind

No one really notices wind until he begins sailing, after which he finds that it varies both in strength and in character. We will not go deeply into meteorology since that is a vast subject, but it is as well to note a few points in passing.

No wind is constant in speed. It blows in gusts which rise and fall. Nor is it constant in direction; it is continually shifting a little. This means that while we are sailing, and in particular sailing close-hauled, the sails are either full or just fluttering and we must steer the boat so that they stay at their proper angle, bearing away and luffing up as required. In the heavy puffs we can bear up a bit, too, and in light airs we must steer by feel as well as by watching the burgee at the masthead. As the wind blows over the water, it will average a particular speed of, say, 10 mph. If our boat is moving forward under engine and dead into it at a speed of perhaps 5 mph, the wind we feel on our face is one of 15 mph. This is known as the "apparent" wind as opposed to the "true" wind and if we are sailing at an angle to the wind, the apparent wind that we feel will have been bent by our forward progress as well as being increased by it (Fig. 18). This sounds very technical perhaps, but it makes sense at sea. It also explains why even a light breeze and warm sunshine ashore can become rather a chilly business at sea. To add further to this complex problem we can mention the effect of the tidal current which, when it is with us, is actually increasing our speed in relation to the true wind. This accounts for many a rough passage on what

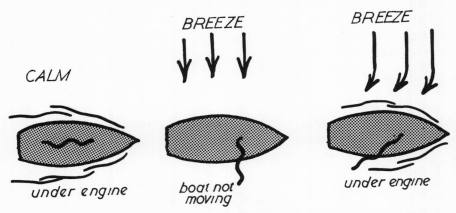

CALM   BREEZE   BREEZE

under engine   boat not moving   under engine

Fig. 18: Apparent wind. In a calm a boat under engine makes her own wind; likewise a drifting boat, not moving forward, is subject to the true wind. If she starts her engine and moves forward (or if she trims her sails and begins sailing) the true wind combined with the wind of her forward motion produces a combined effect known as apparent wind

should have been a hot and balmy day with just a nice little sailing breeze. Our speed, plus a fair tide, plus the true wind speed against us can all add up to "half a gale," or so it seems.

Wind must be studied, shipping forecasts listened to (and a woman remembers forecasts when a man so often forgets them), and signs in the sky heeded all the time when sailing. Wind makes or mars a cruise. Too much and the passage becomes a trial of strength for the crew; too little and, apart from a restful and maybe sun-blessed holiday, time is wasted under engine or just drifting.

The technique of getting from place to place under sail is the whole joy of the business, and can account for the mood the skipper is in. It also involves a good deal of frustration at times, particularly when dying wind, or wind shifting to blow from ahead, coupled with a tide about to turn foul, means the abandonment of plans and maybe long hours of battling just when everybody has had about enough. There is always the engine, of course, but men are funny creatures and feel a sense of injured pride and of "giving in" at the thought of motoring. If a woman understands the fascination of sailing she is less likely to throw a match in the powder barrel by demanding to be motored home. By the same token, she can ease the skipper's wounded pride by talking over the pros and cons with him.

6/Basic Crewing

Getting to grips

One thing is certain: a woman, wife or girl friend never remains a passenger for long. Either by choice or persuasion she begins to play a more active role. Often she learns to do a few simple jobs and, in addition to running the galley, this is the limit of her participation. This is a common state of affairs and it is not altogether wise. Sooner or later an emergency arises, maybe a small one, and the skipper and his other crew (if any) become involved beyond their ability to cope. The woman who can step in quickly, take over the running of the engine, the quick stowage of sails, or the handling of the anchor, turns chaos into order and the emergency into just another exciting incident.

Mooring buoys

As we have seen, once a mooring is let go the boat is free to move and must be given forward power from motor or sails so that she can be steered. Thus it is easy to see that if the buoy is let go too soon the boat may drift straight into another one moored nearby before she can be got under control. Accordingly, the mooring must never be let go until the order is given. Never anticipate this order. Once the mooring buoy has been thrown clear you should sing out "All clear" or something of the sort, so that the man on the helm knows immediately.

The mooring is usually rope (or chain) made fast to a strong cleat or post on the foredeck, and the buoy may be on the end of an extra length of line which lies coiled on deck while the boat is moored, Once in the water, the mooring sinks and the buoy marks it so that it can be picked up again. The mooring must be let go from its post and allowed to run smoothly out over the bow fairlead, and finally the buoy and rope must be *seen to be clear* of everything on deck and thrown clear. Sometimes buoy and rope are thrown clear first and chain last, but if this is done be sure to throw them through the same gap in the rails or pulpit that the chain is led through, otherwise the boat will suddenly bring up with a jerk as the buoy tangles around a stanchion (Fig. 19).

The dinghy has been left on the mooring, which means that this woman has an easy pickup. However, she would have been wise to have the boathook ready in case the helmsman sheered off, or the wind blew the dinghy out of reach

The reason for throwing the buoy clear is that if this is not done, its rope may be caught up by the propeller or, in the case of a twin-keeled yacht, around one of her keels. It is often a wise plan for the crew member forward to point to the cast-off mooring

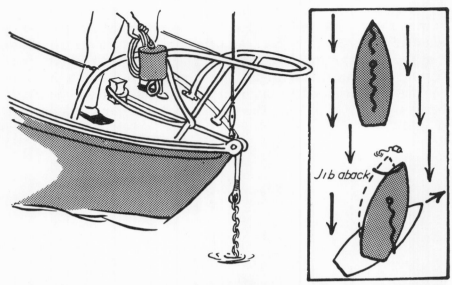

Fig. 19: Letting go the mooring. The buoy and its rope have been led forward and out through the gap in the pulpit by which it originally came in. Failure to do this would mean that when the mooring was dropped the buoy rope might be left hitched round a stanchion

Fig. 20: This diagram shows how a boat's bows are turned in the desired direction by backing the jib just before the mooring is let go

buoy in order that the helmsman can best avoid fouling it.

If the boat is to leave her mooring under sail, the operation is sometimes different and slightly more complicated. She will probably be lying head to wind on the mooring and it may be important that she goes off on, say, port tack (wind blowing on her port side) so that she has room to gather speed and steerage in a clear space of water between other moored boats. This means that the mooring must not be let go while the boat's bows are pointing in the wrong direction. The helmsman may yell out "Let go" but by the time you have got the chain clear the boat may have swung back and be pointing the wrong way. A moment or two later she may have swung again and be facing the right way and *that* is the moment when the mooring must be slipped clear.

In other words the woman on the foredeck must know what the skipper plans to do and be watchful to ensure that she helps him do it. Usually the jib will be backed momentarily so that it pushes the bow in the right direction and this will impede her work somewhat; if she really knows what she's doing she'll be the one to grab the sail and do the backing in an emergency, but more of that later (Fig. 20).

Picking up a mooring is a very different procedure and one which is exclusively a feminine job. Nor is it always an altogether enviable one. The skipper will have tried to handle the boat so that he approaches the mooring buoy very slowly and right on the nose—he is not always successful in this endeavor. He may take a run at it too fast and we are expected to grab it with our boat-hook, haul it aboard and make it fast *before* the full weight

Whatever the job to be tackled on the foredeck, kneel down to it, or better still, sit down to it. Non-slip shoes are essential and a safety harness would not be out of place

of the yacht comes on it! He may misjudge it and the boat stops dead when it is just out of reach—in which case we are expected to have telescopic arms!

Standing on the foredeck, a little to one side so that the skipper can see the buoy, it is possible to sense whether it is to be a good shot or a bad one and to prepare for it. It is sometimes necessary to give directions to the helmsman, who may lose sight of the buoy once it is blacked out by the bows. The best method is simply to point at it. Arms-waving this way or that could be misinterpreted as an instruction to push the tiller one way or the other; pointing leaves nobody in doubt.

The buoy will have a loop of some sort and into this the hook of the boat-hook must go. If you miss, it is often better to hook the buoy rope itself so that the weight of the now dangling buoy allows you to lift it. Either way, get it aboard as fast as you can, especially if the boat is still moving fairly fast. Remember that the buoy must come aboard so that it has a clear run under lifelines, etc. (Fig. 21).

The aim now is to "take a turn." This means that instead of laboriously trying to pull in all the slack and make the chain fast in the full and final manner, enough of the buoy rope is pulled in quickly to wind round the post or cleat two or three times, preferably in a figure 8 manner. The end is then held waiting for the strain to come on it as the yacht continues to move forward until she has reached the end of her tether. Then the buoy rope brings her up, stretches taut and takes the strain until she drops back. By this time, or well before, we hope, the skipper will have joined you on the foredeck and taken over the rest of the operation.

If you miss the buoy, don't go running aft to try for another shot at the stern, especially when under sail. Even if you got it aboard and were able to hold on, the boat would then be moored in such a way as to cause her to swing stern-to-wind under full sail. The result would be a most horrible pantomime. Don't try to hang on to the buoy at risk of being pulled over the side. The skipper's job is to make it possible to get it aboard; if he muffs

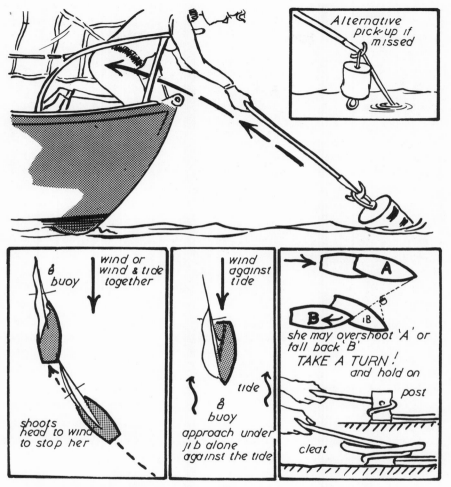

Fig. 21: Hook the buoy as early as possible and get it aboard through the proper gap in the pulpit rails. If the buoy cannot be hooked easily, pick up the rope beneath it (inset). Take a turn. The lower sketches show how a sailing boat usually shoots head to wind in order to stop as close as possible to the buoy, although with wind and tide against each other she may do as shown in the center sketch. Sometimes the yacht may approach too fast and overshoot the buoy—all the more reason for taking a turn as soon as you can, but keep hands a safe distance from the cleat or post

Beating up through a narrow channel means careful navigation and calls for more than a hand holding the tiller. At times like this a wife who can really sail the ship makes all the difference. Note the lifebuoy on the stern locker which can be grabbed from its shock-cord anchor and thrown over the side quickly. The flashing light (stowed upside down because it flashes automatically when up-right) follows on its line and ensures that the buoy is visible during darkness

it, and you have done your honest best, it is better to let him sort his troubles out and come round for another try.

Sail handling

We have taken a fairly close look at the how and why of sailing and a woman's part in crewing, but now we must get still closer to the job.

Each time a boat tacks or jibes, bringing the wind from one side to the other, the sails have to be trimmed across. In the case of the mainsail it may not need touching unless adjustment is needed to harden it in or let it out a bit. When the boat passes the eye of the wind, it swings across automatically. The jib sheets, however, usually must be trimmed across, which means that if, for instance, the boat has the wind blowing on her port side (on the port tack), the starboard (or leeward) jib sheet is in use and the port (or weather) one is slack. As she tacks, the jib shakes and rattles mightily, the starboard sheet is slacked off and the port one hauled in.

In light breezes this is an easy job soon mastered, but in fresher winds muscle power alone is not enough and so the sheet winches begin to earn their keep. These winches are so designed that they will revolve in one direction only. The sheet is wound round the barrel three to four times, in the direction which allows the winch to revolve as the sheet is pulled in. A lever handle is then used to turn the winch until the sheet is considered tight enough.

There is a knack to it, but it doesn't take long to master and in mastering it most of the hard work is avoided. Let us sum up by imagining a tack being made. The boat is tramping along close-hauled and the skipper says, "Right, we'd better go about." The correct order is then, "Ready about," when the crew loosens the end of the sheet from the cleat near the leeward winch, but without allowing it to slacken off the winch itself. "Ready," she says. "Hard a-lee!" comes the order as the skipper puts the tiller across. The crew uncleats the sheet, spins the turns off the winch, takes a quick glance to make sure that nothing is liable to snag, and takes hold of the new lee sheet. As the boat comes nose to wind she begins to pull in the slack sheet and then winds it quickly (and in the correct direction) round the winch. She pulls in as much of the slack as she can while the sail is still flapping, causing the winch to spin merrily. At the very moment when the sails fill with wind on the new tack she will be using the handle to winch in the last couple of feet of sheet to harden the sail well in. Finally she makes the end of the sheet fast to its cleat, without losing any of her hard-won tension in the process (Fig. 22).

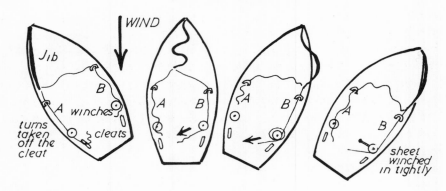

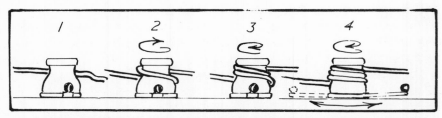

Fig. 22: Working the sheet winches. The diagram shows the stages of a boat tacking from starboard to port tack. The sheet to leeward is released as she comes around and the new lee sheet gathered in slowly so that the sail is not backed. A turn is taken around the winch (third sketch) as the jib begins to fill and the slack sheet is spun in as fast as possible. More turns must be put on the winch before the full load of the sail develops and the rest of the slack winched in by means of the handle. Bottom sketches show a winch in action. As soon as there is a load on it the slack end of the rope must be held tightly while winching in or the turns will fail to grip. Most winches on American boats have their handles at the top of the winch in order that the handle can be turned entirely around through 360 degrees without the cranker's arm striking the sheet

The mainsheet doesn't pose much of a problem. It is arranged so that the work is made easy by the use of blocks, and it is usually the helmsman's job to adjust it since he is nearest to it in a small sailboat. However, it is as well to know just what effect the mainsail has on the steering because there are times when the mainsheet needs to be slackened off quickly and hauled in equally fast.

In most small vessels the mainsail tends to make the boat turn

Surging

Ⓐ

Ⓑ

Ⓒ *KEEP HANDS WELL CLEAR*

Fig. 23: Surging rope or chain. When rope or chain is under tension and made fast it sometimes has to be slacked off. If this is done unguardedly it can take charge. A flat-of-hand method for ropes on winches is shown in B

into the eye of the wind and the jib counteracts it. Thus, if it is necessary to make the boat turn quickly *away* from the wind —to bear away, in fact, the mainsheet must be let out a little if it was previously trimmed hard in. In sudden emergency, when the skipper has his hands full and is trying to bear away, a quick-thinking crew would jump for the mainsheet and let it go for him. Our old friend the jibe is another case for smart mainsheet handling.

Running before the wind, with the mainsail right out, a jibe, and the consequent crossing of the mainsail from one side to the other, means that, as it swings over, the sheet will be momentarily slack unless it is hauled in smartly and then let out again as the sail swings over. A slack sheet can lasso the helmsman or foul up on a projection. It also allows the boom to flip up and perhaps become hooked against the backstay—causing a total loss of control of the boat.

The knack, in a fresh breeze anyhow, is to haul in the slack sheet quickly and then take a turn until the main shock of the boom has passed, letting the sheet run out again under control by "surging" it around the cleat. This may sound technical, but it is really quite simple when demonstrated (Fig. 23).

Setting and stowing sails

In the modern small sailboat there are very few lines (ropes) to
be handled. Sheets we have already identified, but there are also
the halyards (haulyards in olden days), by means of which the
sails are raised or lowered, and downhauls or tack tackles used
for tensioning sails downwards after they have been hauled up
on the halyards and made fast (Fig. 24). Finally there is the
topping lift, which simply holds up the end of the boom.

We have all raised and lowered a clothesline in our time and
the raising and lowering of sails is not so very different. The main
difference is that the sails flapping in the wind are a bit
frightening; their sheets lash around and the sail itself needs
watching, as it goes aloft, to ensure that it doesn't snag up on
some part of the rigging and perhaps tear. In fact a flogging sail
is 90 percent noise and nothing to be frightened of. In bad weather
it is rather different because a sail out of control is powerful; if
one keeps up-wind of it, however, it need not be dangerous to
handle.

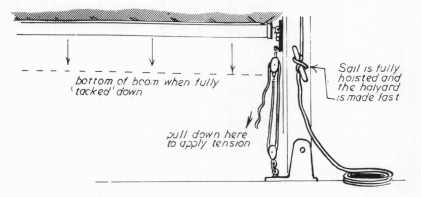

Fig. 24: Tacking down the mainsail. Not all yachts have this arrangement, but most modern ones do. By tacking down in this way the
tension on the luff of the sail can be varied. In fresh winds it is
tacked down as hard as possible to flatten the sail; slacking it
makes the sail shape fuller for light airs and this moves the draft or
belly further aft

Some women sail for years with their husbands and yet never venture out of the cockpit. Usually, in anything of a breeze, it is right that it should be this way because the changing of headsails, reefing during a squall, securing things which are washing adrift, and so on, are best left to the men; having had more practice they are much faster, as a rule. Also a woman can best help by remaining in charge of the helm, so long as she knows what she is about. It is wrong, however, to confine a woman to the cockpit for all time. Sooner or later she will have to cope on deck, so ideally she should get her practice during reasonable weather, learning the knack of sail-changing and so on.

First and foremost comes the matter of safety, and the need to exercise great care when moving around on deck. (We'll be discussing man-overboard action later.) One goes forward on the uphill side if the yacht is heeling—and usually she is if under sail. There may be above knee-high lifelines along the sides of the deck, though all sailboats are not fitted with them. Either way it is best to behave as if they were not there at all and keep a firm grip on the wooden grab-rails on the cabin top, on the rigging, the mast, and so on. It is no bad plan to wear a safety harness at first even in calm weather, and always in rough weather or at night.

Once at the job to be done sit down to work. This is the safest of all methods and nobody will laugh because it is a mark of the expert—in rough weather certainly. Either sit or kneel, but sit for preference and clip on the harness hook to rail or rigging.

Sails are usually set in quiet waters, either on the mooring or while motoring down-river towards the open sea. The main is usually the first to be set and the boat will be brought head to wind if possible, or at least heading in such a way that the sail is empty of wind and shaking. You hoist it right up, being sure to look aloft to see that all is well as it goes up its track, whereupon the halyard is made fast to its cleat. The downhaul is set up and the halyard is coiled neatly (see later section on handling lines) and hung on its cleat (Fig. 25).

The procedure is similar for the jib or genoa—if lighter winds call for this larger type of jib—except that it may have to be hanked on to the stay. We won't dwell on this operation since it will call for a practical demonstration if it is to be tackled by the crew. However, be sure that no hanks are twisted, that the sail is not snagged round, say, the anchor, and that the sheets are clear to run and the halyard clipped on after a look aloft to ensure that it is not twisted around the forestay. One word of warning. The sheets may be attached to the sail by means of a patent clip-hook and when the sail is flogging around this hard metal fitting can inflict a painful blow or smash glasses—so beware!

Now and then sail needs to be set while the yacht is pitching and rolling around at anchor and while the skipper may be occupied with other things. It may also have to be done in the

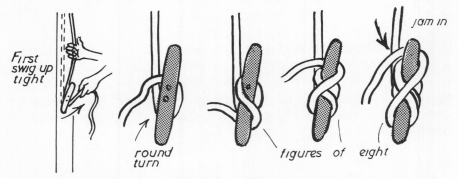

Fig. 25: Making a halyard fast. Slack line is swigged up, one hand holding the cleat end while the other swigs down the slack line from aloft. A full turn is taken around the cleat, then figures-of-eight turns. The end of the halyard is jammed in tight against the upright or "standing" part of the halyard. Some people finish off with a half-hitch, but this should only be used with synthetic rope which does not swell and jam when wet

dark and conditions may be such that a woman has to tackle the job on her own. Knowing the ropes and the drill is what matters then.

The stowing of sails also calls for skill. The skipper may have his hands full maneuvering the boat under engine in a tricky spot and he may call for the sails to be lowered. It is simple enough to let go the halyards, but not always so simple to get the sails down if they are filled with wind. This means that they must be pulled down by hand and will balloon and flog around like mad. All the time they are ballooning and flogging they are restricting the helmsman's view, so speed at this time is essential. (Here incidentally a word of warning—never stand on Dacron sails; they are extremely slippery.) After subduing sails a sail stop will have to be used to hold them temporarily. The wise woman will have stuffed a couple of these canvas strips (some boats have different methods) in her jacket or pocket before going forward and she can now pass them round the sail and its boom, or the sail and its stay if it is a jib, and tie them with a reef knot (see knots, hitches, and bends). If the skipper has not already done so, she must then hasten aft and take in the slack of the mainsheet to stop the now sail-less boom from crashing around.

At the helm

There is a great deal of difference between "holding the tiller" under strict instructions to put it this way or that and "taking the helm." A woman who can take the helm under sail or power and on any particular point of sailing, beating, reaching, running, etc., and under any conditions of wind and sea, immediately gives her skipper freedom to navigate with care or do other essential jobs. Unless he can be sure that the boat will be sailed safely and properly he will devote only half his mind to what he ought to be doing, and the consequences could be serious if he made a mistake.

A woman crew who has sailed a dinghy will not need to be told that a tiller seems to work backwards. If it is swung to the left the bow of the boat will go to the right and vice versa. This apparent paradox makes sense when a boat is under sail and heeling over. We forget about left and right or port and starboard and think in terms of up and down. Imagine the yacht to be heeling and sailing along. You are sitting on the uphill or windward side with the wind blowing on that side. If you pull

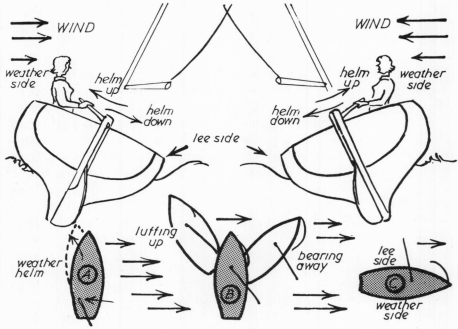

Fig. 26: These sketches show how weather side and lee side are unrelated to port and starboard—the "windy" side is the weather or windward side. At A the yacht has a natural tendency to steer herself into the wind and the tiller is kept "up" (upwind) a little to counteract this. B shows the difference between luffing up and bearing away, changes of course entirely related to the direction of the wind and irrespective of port or starboard. At C the boat is running before the wind, but there is still a lee and a weather side, according to which side the boom is on

the tiller towards you it will be coming up, i.e. towards the wind. If you push it away from you it will be going down or away from the wind. Only when a boat is on a dead run before the wind does this ruling cease to apply (Fig. 26).

Under sail, beating or reaching or doing anything other than a dead run, the "feel" of the tiller is directly related to the effect of the sails. As we have seen, the force of the mainsail tends to make the boat want to turn her nose up into the wind and in order to prevent her doing this there is the effect of the jib to balance her. As a boat heels and the wind strengthens, however, she tends to exert more and more of her willpower, so to speak. If the tiller is let go most boats will automatically slew round, until they are head to wind. Some boats have this tendency to a strong degree and are said to be "hard headed"; others are better balanced due to sails and hull shape and have very little, if any, of this "weather helm" as it is called. Most small family sailboats have it to some degree. It is not really a bad thing and, in fact, it is a built-in safety device (when the weather helm is moderate). It is easier to get the feel of such boats. When at the tiller the helmsman feels it pulling against him gently. To make the boat turn away from the wind he pulls against the pull, and if he wants to head up into the wind a little he allows the tiller to have its own way a shade—letting it get away from him or *down* a bit.

As explained earlier the wind is never quite constant, in strength or in direction; consequently the helmsman is continuously pulling and easing his tiller to keep the boat on course or to keep the sails full of wind. If sailing close-hauled, for instance, the wind may head him a shade so that the jib begins to flutter. Instantly he pulls the tiller *up* and bears away a few degrees until the sail just stops fluttering. Conversely the wind may free just a little so that he can, if he wishes, sail even closer to the wind, therefore he puts his tiller *down* a shade.

Usually a woman crew who doesn't yet know how to sail by the wind, as we say, is told to "steer for that buoy" or whatever the mark may be. Accordingly she keeps the bows pointed at it and moves the tiller to suit. The knack is to use the tiller as little as possible. Wide sweeping movements (which she will make at first) are soon tailored down to the imperceptible give-and-take tiller technique. She must beware of getting right off course and panicking. She might then begin see-sawing around, whereupon the boat will swerve and swoop and the sails will flap loudly. She should remember that *the boat will want to go one way more than the other.*

Under engine, life is less tricky although usually a single-screwed boat will also try to wander off course. This is due to the side-paddling effect of the propeller, but it is very slight at low speeds and soon summed up.

The woman on the helm, with her husband working on deck forward, must be ready for the sudden extra puff of wind which makes the boat heel far over. If this happens she can luff up a shade, pointing the bows a little nearer to the eye of the wind so that some of the weight of the wind is shed. Alternatively, and if circumstances merit it, she can ease out a few feet of mainsheet so that the wind is spilled. If the man forward is trying to change the jib he will bless the woman who can gentle the boat along without deluging him with spray and making his job more difficult—providing, and it is an important point, she doesn't overdo the luffing and tack the boat round altogether.

In passing it should be mentioned that the engine controls, although extremely simple compared to those of a car, should be understood by the woman on the helm. Usually, in any modern craft, there will be a button for starting the engine and a switch of some kind to stop it. There will also be an ahead/astern lever and an accelerator, or throttle, as it is called. The system is that the engine is never banged from full ahead to full astern. It should first be slowed down, then the lever moved through neutral into the other gear and the throttle opened again. Be sure the fuel line valve is open and the bilge blower is run to exhaust gas fumes before the engine is started.

Giving orders—and taking them

The biggest bone of contention aboard a yacht often lies in the orders, vocal and visual, given by the skipper to the helmswoman. It is worth getting this clear right from the start. When a man gestures to the right, for instance, does he mean that he wants the bows of the yacht to go that way or does he want the tiller pushed in the direction indicated? Likewise, when he yells "Port a bit," does he mean bows or tiller? The odds are that he wants the tiller pushed when he gestures and the bows turned when he shouts! Obviously this is something to sort out right from the start to avoid a scene. There may be moments when it isn't so easy to remember which is port or starboard. Remember the *aide mémoire* "Jack left port" and that port wine is red. Thus the navigation lights are red to port and green to starboard.

In these early stages of learning to be at home afloat, much is perplexing and even worrying. A small yacht really moves very slowly, probably never faster than 8 mph unless she is a fast power cruiser. For all that, even under sail, there is a great deal of noise of rushing water and flapping canvas, and things happen at breakneck speed. Small emergencies—which certainly do not threaten life or limb—crop up out of the blue and a man is apt to thrust the tiller, or a line, into his woman's hands and expect her to cope, somehow.

Keeping calm is essential. A calm woman makes a panicking man feel foolish, providing she is not just calm because she is so green that she is unaware of any crisis. Very often a man will school himself to keep calm for the general good of all concerned, simply because he has a woman looking on. If he does so right from the beginning of a sailing relationship, don't let him lose the habit. Never permit tantrums. Don't nag, but keep calm and allow him to feel foolish if he must. He'll soon master his tantrum. A lot of tact is needed all round when it comes to taking orders which have been given in a moment of frantic uncertainty. A man may be in a bit of a mood and infuriating as a consequence, but the orders he gives may be urgent and to ignore them "just to show him who's who" could easily lead to real trouble, possibly involving risk to human life. Difficult though it may be at the time, *always* obey first and skin him alive later, when there is time to spare.

Anchor work

The anchor has been the symbol of hope since early times and it remains, very often, the last recourse of the small yacht in a tight spot. An anchor is designed to dig into the bottom or seabed and either to continue to dig down the harder the yacht tugs on her cable or to lie with one arm and fluke spiked in firmly. If the strain becomes very great the anchor will either drag, bury

Fig. 27: If the scope or length of cable paid out is too short the anchor will fail to bite. The minimum safe scope is three times the depth of water at high water in the anchorage, but more will be needed in strong winds or if the seabed is poor holding ground. The three typical anchors shown are (A), Fisherman, a non-burying type; (B) Danforth or Meon, burying anchor; (C) plow or CQR type, also burying. (D) shows a Danforth at its normal depth in soft sand or mud

deeper, or rise to the surface of the seabed, and then dig in and bury again.

This is a great simplification of what happens to both the plough type and Danforth type buriers and the surface-holding Fisherman types of anchor. In all cases an anchor depends for its hold upon the type of seabed, its size, weight, type, and suitability for the ship, and the length of anchor cable paid out. The length of cable needed is from three times the deepest depth of water in fair weather (tides rise and fall, remember) to five times, but never less than three times and more if space to swing on the tide without hitting nearby boats allows. In a real gale and in an exposed anchorage yachts may have to let out eight or more times the depth of water to prevent them dragging (Fig. 27).

From this it can be seen that an anchorage must be chosen with care and it is no use complaining if the skipper anchors in a spot which is a long row from the landing place ashore. Safety first, convenience second. It is also easy to see that anchors must be let go carefully so that they are not buried under a heap of chain, which might tangle with them and prevent them working properly (Fig. 28). While the skipper may have to concentrate on finding the ideal spot where there is room for the yacht to swing as the tide or the wind changes direction, it is often the wife's

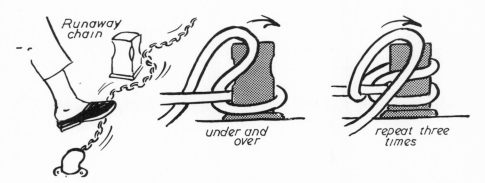

Runaway chain

under and over

repeat three times

Fig. 28: If the yacht is anchored in deep water the chain may run out too fast and pile up on top of the anchor in a tangle. Never grab a runaway chain, stamp on it. Rope or chain cable should never be made fast in a way which could tighten and be difficult to let go. The tug-boat hitch shown is the correct way and it is safe and easy to cast off, especially with chain

job to let go the anchor precisely where he wants it. Remember the spot where the anchor goes down is not the position in which the yacht will finally lie; she will end up some distance downwind or down current of it.

When the order to "let go" is given the anchor must be allowed to drop to the seabed quickly. This means that perhaps three to five fathoms (18 to 30 feet) of chain, or rope, must be allowed to run out at once (according to the depth, which is something you should expect to be told). Thereafter the cable is allowed to run out slowly as the yacht drifts back on wind or current. (Fig. 29).

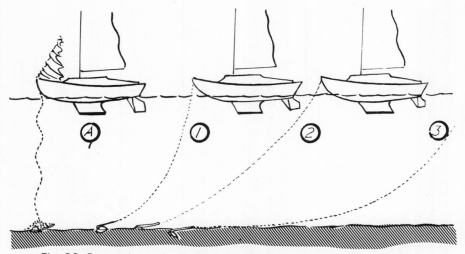

Fig. 29: Stages in anchoring. At A the chain has been allowed to run out too fast and it has piled up on top of the anchor, possibly preventing it from working properly. At 1 the yacht is allowed to drift astern while chain is paid out smoothly and at 2 it is held by taking a turn or snubbing it to make the anchor take a bite. At 3 the yacht is out of sight but the anchor is beginning to bury itself safely

It is dangerous to throw an anchor overboard. It must be passed out under the rail at the bows and over the fairlead and simply released, either from the hands or by letting it dangle on its chain and releasing the chain or rope at the right moment. To throw an anchor is risky. A turn of cable could get round an ankle, with heaven knows what consequences, or it could become fouled up in its cable and refuse to work properly on the seabed.

Anchor cables are, or should be, marked at intervals of five fathoms so that it is possible to see at a glance how much length has been let out. The usual method of anchoring is to let go, then pay out two or three ship's lengths of cable and "snub" it. This seemingly anti-social word means simply that the cable is held by taking a turn on a cleat or post just long enough to straighten it out under tension for a second or two. The rest of the scope (required length according to depth of water) is then let out and finally made fast properly, or "for a full due," as the saying goes. Sometimes an owner likes to go astern on the engine to give it a good tug so that the point of the anchor digs home.

If there is a lot of wind and the yacht charges astern and brings up hard on her cable it is as well to watch for a while to ensure that she is not dragging. Look ashore and get any two marks (a tree on the shore and a distant house in the background, for instance) in line. If the yacht is dragging, the marks will soon come out of line and the gap will steadily widen. This means that more anchor scope is needed, or that she just isn't going to hold at all and a fresh anchorage is needed (Fig. 30).

Sometimes anchoring is a hectic business. In a fresh wind, a bit of a lumpy sea and maybe darkness and rain, a woman just may have to do the letting go if her man is so involved at his

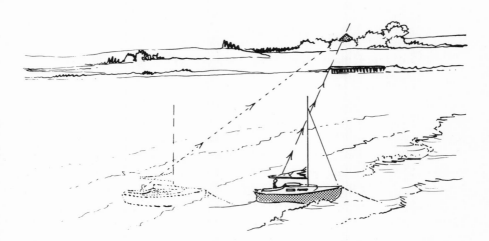

Fig. 30: The observer in this yacht has taken marks ashore to see if she is dragging the anchor; the end of the jetty in line with the house gable. The dotted line boat shows how these marks would "open" if she had dragged. Note: in gusts of strong wind there would be a bit of give and take causing the marks to shift in and out of line a small amount, and also the yacht's swinging to wind shifts would alter the range

The anchorage must be chosen carefully. When the yacht finally lies back on her anchor, she must have room to swing and must be clear of deep water channels. The important thing is that when the order to "let go" is given the anchor must be dropped quickly

tiller that he can't do both jobs. In such a case, when it is vital perhaps that the anchor bites first time and holds, the first essential is to be sure that the cable will run smoothly up from its locker below without kinking, jamming or in any way preventing the anchor from doing its job. While the yacht is running towards the chosen anchorage, haul about five fathoms of cable up on deck and then let it run back again or else let it remain on deck neatly coiled—this will clear any kinks.

In such circumstances the letting go will have to be done with great care to avoid the risk of injury. Everything will be heaving and crashing around and the boat will drift astern at great speed too—maybe off at an angle in a great clamor of shaking sails. The cable will have to be paid out very quickly and snubbing may have to be left until the full scope is out. What is important is that the final turns are taken before the weight of the ship comes on the cable. Once she lies back on the cable it will twang taut viciously and this can be dangerous to anyone who doesn't know what to expect. The best method is to pile three or four turns round the post and let her snub herself, then, when the cable slackens momentarily, the making fast part can be completed. In all probability, by this time the skipper will have taken over, but it is as well to know the drill.

At anchor, a yacht keeps up a series of swings and surges to and fro. At the turn of the tide, the cable slackens and is dragged over the seabed before pulling from the opposite direction, and at every sudden change of wind the yacht alters the direction of the pull. All this means that anyone asleep below is subjected to a series of rumbles and clankings, if the cable is a chain one, and it is easy to imagine that the anchor is dragging, as perhaps it is. I have always had a keen ear for a dragging anchor and

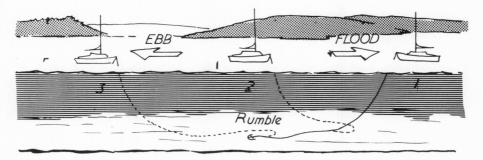

Fig. 31: The alarming rumbles heard while anchored at night are usually caused by the chain dragging over itself at turn of the tide. At 1 the yacht is lying to the flood. At 2 the ebb is carrying her downstream over her anchor and the chain is rumbling. At 3 she is riding to the ebb and quiet again. If wind and current are in opposition she may sheer around and rumble half the night. Rope anchor cables almost completely obviate this noise

have turned my grumbling husband out at night on several occasions and been proved right (Fig. 31).

Don't on the other hand, take up a "burglars in the kitchen" attitude. With experience you will learn what a dragging anchor

Fig. 32: Stages in breaking out. Cable is shortened up until it is
up-and-down, whereupon the anchor loses hold and breaks out

really sounds like. The best way is to go and look, either at marks
in line or at the cable. A dragging ship usually tightens her cable
as she strains on it, then drags it with a rumble, whereupon it
goes slack, then tightens and rumbles again and so on. This
sequence also happens at times when she has just swung and is
taking up slack, so don't be fooled. Place a hand on the cable
and feel the tension and the rumble. By lying below, knowing
the state of the wind and the tide and listening, a fair idea of
what to expect can be gained.

All this is perhaps best left to the skipper until you have more
experience. Remember though that to know is to be ready for
the unexpected and that all boat knowledge is useful some time.
More to the point is the drill for getting the anchor in. If the
elements have combined to make this a physically difficult job
it is really a man's responsibility and he'll want it so, but now
and then it becomes a woman's job—maybe in a slight emergency.
The golden rule is to let the ship do the hardest work. Either
she will be motored towards the anchor position while slack chain
is hauled in, or it will be gathered in in a series of easy hauls,
waiting each time as the yacht strains back at it, taking a quick
turn perhaps meanwhile. Once you have started the boat moving
forward, continue to haul just hard enough to keep her going,
paying the cable down its pipe into the locker as you go.

In due course the cable will come "up and down," which is
self-explanatory (Fig. 32). If the anchor is firmly dug in it may
be necessary to take a turn so that the weight of the yacht moving
forward can snub its hold loose from the seabed. As soon as the
hold breaks the boat is free to get under way and in many cases
there is not much time to waste in getting going and under proper
control, so the skipper must be told at once. The rest of the job

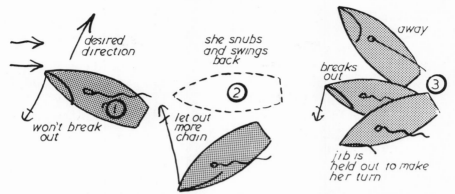

Fig. 33: Breaking out under sail when the anchor refuses to let go. It is essential that the yacht pays off and begins moving (in this case towards the top of the page, or on port tack) in the desired direction. At 1 she refuses and the jerk of the cable turns her bow the wrong way. At 2 a little more cable is let go so that she does not break out and sail in the wrong direction. In 3 the jib is backed and slack cable gathered in quickly as she swings back yet again, and this time the anchor breaks out correctly

entails hauling up the anchor and getting it aboard carefully without banging hull or paintwork. It must then be washed off and lashed down on its chocks.

In the section on letting go moorings we stressed that it is often important to see that the boat is free to sail off in the desired direction—on one tack or the other, in fact. This is fairly easy to do when letting go a mooring, but at anchor it is not so simple. The anchor must not be broken out while the boat is heading in the wrong direction. Very likely the mainsail and the jib will be set—the latter belaboring you as it flogs around. The trick is to get the cable nearly up and down, then "back" the jib against the wind so that it forces the yacht's bows in the desired direction. The cable is then quickly hauled in and the anchor out in one movement (Fig. 33). If by any chance it doesn't break its hold, the yacht will probably swing back on the wrong tack again. In which case, wait until she completes her swing. It may even be necessary to let go a bit more chain, temporarily, just to hold her until she swings back again in the right direction. The second shot should be successful.

Since anchors dig deep into muddy seabeds and are often dirty when they come up, wear gloves to protect hands from this and from the rough ironwork, and trying to keep the worst of the mud from coming on board. A nylon bristle pan brush attached to a stick about two feet long is useful. By leaving the anchor hanging just out of the water it is easy to reach over and scrub off the worst of the mud before lifting it aboard or, if the anchor is not too heavy, dunking it up and down a few times will remove most of the mud.

Handling lines

In any small sailboat lines need to be handled and the easiest way to spot a beginner is to see him, or her, pick up a coil of rope. The crux of the matter is the word "coil." The only way a line can be picked up and remain ready for use is in a coil, otherwise it becomes a tangle. The experienced yachtsman cannot tolerate a line that is not coiled and his first instinctive reaction is to coil it, or if it has been coiled badly, to re-coil it.

There are all sorts of ropes, usually called lines, in a yacht. Halyards, when the sails are set, offer a mass of slack line on deck; mainsheets become a muddle in the cockpit and so does the lee jib sheet, which also creates a lot of slack end to lie around. Then there are warps for mooring or anchoring, heaving lines (more about them later) and many more shorter bits and pieces of rope. If lines are not tidy and an emergency crops up, chaos soon reigns. An untidy, loose end can fall overboard and get wrapped around the propeller, for instance, or a sheet become knotted which prevents the sail from being let out—perhaps during a squall when it has become vital to spill wind.

Certain types of rope are easier to coil than others, but the standing rule with all ordinary rope laid right-handed is to coil it clockwise. Imagine taking the end of a rope and laying it on the floor in a circle, feeding the rope round in the same direction as the hands of a clock—this is the way to coil a big, heavy warp. Now imagine picking up the coil and holding it in the left hand and continuing to make circles with the right, turn after turn until the rope is coiled (Fig. 34).

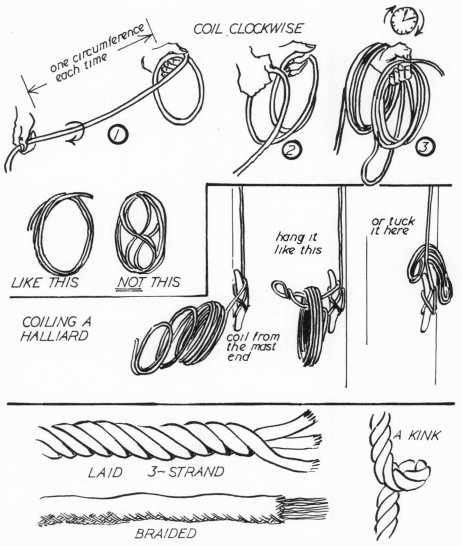

Fig. 34: Coiling. It is essential to develop a mechanical hand movement when coiling lines. Each turn should lie naturally over the previous one if the rope is free of twists and kinks. The lower sketches show examples of laid 3-strand rope and braided rope. Any kink in a rope like this must be removed at once. It could easily jam and stop a sail being lowered or a sheet eased out

Depending on the thickness of the rope the size, or diameter, of the coil is varied. A small coil, about the size of a dinner plate, is about right for a rope as thick as a pencil, with progressively bigger coils for thicker rope. The aim is to make the smallest coil to which the rope will *naturally* lend itself. The halyards and sheets in a small sailboat will be about half an inch thick and the best coil will be about twelve inches in diameter, though this is a very wide generality. Incidentally, the end of a halyard or sheet which is in use is not coiled from its idle end. It must be coiled straight from where it is attached to its cleat.

Rope may be three-strand stuff or plaited. Nowadays it will almost certainly be of nylon or Dacron, or some other synthetic, and although it is easier to handle and kinder on the hands than old fashioned hemp, manila, or sisal, it can still get kinked. A kink, as everyone knows, is a sharp twist which results from a bit of a tangle or from a coil which has got itself round the wrong way. It's worth knowing that if a kink is allowed to stay in a rope, and that rope comes under a sudden heavy strain, the actual strength at that point can be reduced by half. This means that when rope is coiled all the kinks must be removed from it. Coiling three-strand "right-handed" or twisted rope the wrong way (anti-clockwise) actually puts kinks into it, by the way. The knack is to take the coil in the left hand and build up the turns with the right hand, occasionally giving the slack rope a spin to remove the kinks as they appear.

One of the surest tests of a well coiled line is when the coil has to be thrown or "heaved." If the yacht is maneuvering to go alongside a quay, perhaps, the moment will come when she is near enough for a line to be thrown to the shore. Very few women ever get around to learning how to do this simple, but essential, job. Usually a line is thrown which travels a few feet and then falls in the water hopelessly tangled, by which time the helmsman is pleading for patience and in a fair way to make a mess of the operation himself. This usually results from a rope not being properly coiled in the first place and not properly thrown.

A "heaving line" is a light, supple rope, perhaps 40 feet long, and it may have a big fancy knot or "monkey's fist" at one end to help its progress through the air. Whether it has or not, it must be coiled small—dinner plate size or larger—but according to thickness, and be free of all kinks and twists. When it is to be thrown, the thrower takes the coil in the left hand and divides it so that half the coil and the knot, if there is one, is now in the right hand. The coil must be divided exactly right. The thrower makes sure she has a clear deck behind her and that she has her feet well braced, then swings the throwing arm back

Dividing the coil for a leadline sounding. Remember to make the end fast, otherwise it could all go overboard

and heaves the half coil up and away. If all goes well the airborne coil extends smoothly and the rest of the coil, held loosely in the left hand, remember, follows turn upon turn. The end must be held, of course, and to be on the safe side it is best to stand on it or hitch it around something on deck (Fig. 35).

While on the subject of going alongside, we'll finish dealing with the use of lines for this purpose. If the line has been heaved and caught by someone ashore, the skipper will probably ask him to make it fast or take a turn round a post, or ring. The yacht will have been going ahead and now the skipper may put the engine astern to slow her. Either way, the line will be used to stop her

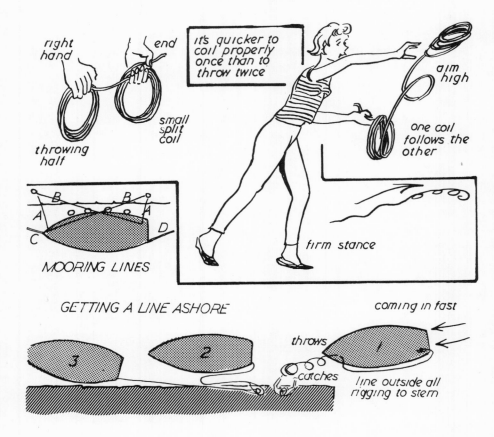

right hand   end   it's quicker to coil properly once than to throw twice

aim high

small split coil

one coil follows the other

throwing half

MOORING LINES

firm stance

GETTING A LINE ASHORE

coming in fast

3   2   throws   1

catches   line outside all rigging to stern

Fig. 35: Careful coiling is the secret when throwing a heaving line. Divide the coil as shown and remember to aim high. There's a knack to throwing a line and it needs practice

The mooring diagram below shows the breast lines (A and A), forward and after springs (B and B) and bow and stern lines (C and D). Moored in this way a boat will lie parallel to the dock even with a current running past or a wind from ahead or astern. When approaching a dock try to get the stern line fast first, if there is going to be difficulty in slowing the yacht. If it is made fast aft and led outside all rigging to the bow and thrown ashore from there, it will give the man ashore more time for making fast before the strain comes on it

progress. In a small sailboat the heaving line will also serve as
a warp for the stopping purpose, but in a bigger boat it would
be used to send a much thicker rope to the man ashore, who hauls
in the thin line to get at the thick one.

Once the line is made fast ashore, you will be told to take it
to the bow or the stern, quickly. What is vital is that the end
must be passed under the rail and in through one of the chocks
and thence to a big enough cleat or post on deck. This must be
done and a turn taken before the strain comes on the rope. If
the boat is moving too fast it is necessary to "surge" the turn,
which means that the turns round the post or cleat are allowed
to slip around a little. This eases the load on the line, which might
otherwise be enough to snap it. Sometimes, in a real panic, there
may not be time to pass the line under the rail properly, in which
case the urgent thing is to stop the headway by taking that turn.
Fingers must be kept well clear, or they could get damaged. Once
the ship has been checked the procedure for mooring up follows,
passing various ropes and lines from ship to shore. This is one
of those techniques best learned by helping a time or two.

Knots, hitches, and bends

You cannot get away with even the most basic crewing for long
without learning at least one or two knots, hitches, or bends. We
generalize wrongly by calling them all "knots," just as we speak
of "tying" them instead of "making fast," but this is perhaps the
counsel of perfection.

Let us content ourselves with learning just six knots (I cannot
keep up this knots, hitches, and bends business): the reef knot,
bowline, figure 8, round turn and two half-hitches, sheet bend,
and clove hitch. Of these the reef knot, figure 8, and round turn
and two half-hitches will take precedence, but for good and useful
crewing all should be known (Fig. 36).

Just as important as knowing how to make the knots is to know
when to use them. The reef knot is for joining the ends of two
lines of equal thickness, and like the rest of the correct knots
it has the virtue of being easy to untie. Incidentally, a point about

knots in synthetic rope: don't make them with the very ends of the lines. This type of rope is limp and slippery and knots are liable to slip easily and quite accidentally. If the knots are vitally important—say in the case of a line made fast (or bent on, as we say) to an anchor, make extra sure by also tying the end to the main line with a piece of string. This is known as "seizing the end."

The bowline is a loop or "bight" which will not slip and it is used in the end of a line or warp which goes over a bollard or post for mooring the boat to a quay, etc. The figure 8 is a "stopper" knot and used at the end of both jib sheets so that they can't be jerked out of their fairleads. It is easy to untie in a hurry and makes a nice big knob. When a rope, such as a dinghy painter

(Opposite.) Fig. 36: THE VITAL KNOTS AND HITCHES

Reef knot: Used for joining two ropes of equal thickness. Be sure that the short ends finish on the same side. Right over left and left over right is the method

Figure 8: Used as a stopper knot to prevent the jib sheets from flipping out of the fairleads. It is easy to untie

Round turn and two half-hitches: A round turn means that the rope goes round the post completely and the half-hitches are made in the same direction each time. Used for making a dinghy fast to a jetty, etc.

Bowline: A loop which will not slip and which can always be untied easily. Used for putting in the end of a mooring line or for joining two warps, one bowline linked through the other. Make the eye part as shown and leave plenty of spare end when the knot is completed

Sheet bend: A joining knot, especially if the two ropes are of different thicknesses. The loop is always made in the thicker rope and the ends finish as shown. Pull the parts of the knot tight carefully as it can dissolve into a muddle if not watched

Clovehitch: For securing a rope's end to a post when the pull is to be a steady one. Tends to tighten, needing strong fingers to slacken it later. It can be made by passing the end round and round then through or by dropping two turns one over the other

In general: Knots, hitches, and bends made in synthetic ropes come undone more easily than those made in natural fiber ropes—in fact they can untie themselves. To guard against this always leave a good long slack end and always pull tight. Never make knots in chain or wire. Use the right knot for the right purpose

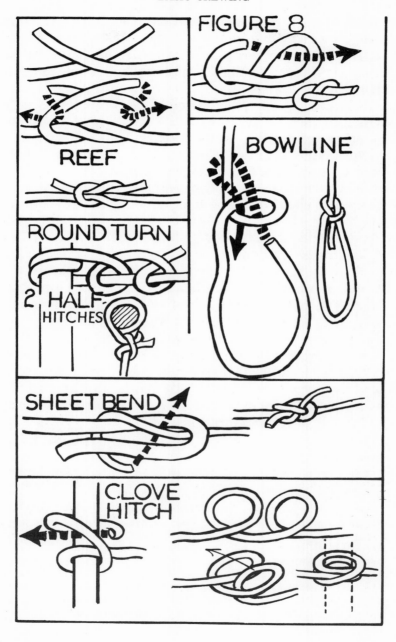

FIGURE 8

REEF

BOWLINE

ROUND TURN

2 HALF-HITCHES

SHEET BEND

CLOVE HITCH

or bow line, has to be made fast to the yacht or to a jetty, the round turn and two half-hitches is the safest and easiest knot to use. Usually it becomes a half turn and two half-hitches, but the important thing is that the hitches are both made in the same direction.

The sheet bend is for joining the end of two ropes of different thickness as a rule. Be sure to use the thicker end as shown and not the other way round, or the knot will fail. If the ropes are very different in thickness, it's best to be on the safe side and make a double sheet bend. The clove hitch is often used instead of the round turn when securing the dinghy, but again don't make it in the very end of the line. It could work its way round and slip.

Overhand knots, the over and under knot, should never be used as they are difficult to untie and anyway they serve no purpose. On the other hand they often appear accidentally in coils of rope and should be undone at once before they tighten up. Another traditionally forbidden knot is the half-hitch by itself used on a cleat. Once the rope comes under strain the hitch just cannot be undone. Even with two or three turns of rope made fast figure 8 fashion around the cleat beforehand, the half hitch should not be used with natural fiber ropes. When these get wet they swell and the hitch jams. Incidentally synthetic ropes don't swell, which brings us to the exception to the rule. In modern yachts, many of which have cleats that are rather small, synthetic rope tends to come undone and now and again a half hitch to hold the turns in place is an advantage.

Practice the knots in thick rope and thin and learn how to tie them blindfold—sooner or later they will have to be made in the dark! Learn to heave a line and coil a rope quickly and know which knots to use and you will be regarded with respect by all sailing men-folk.

The leadline

We've all heard of "swinging the lead." Years ago in big sailing ships it was very hard work to swing the lead and men used to cheat by swinging it, letting it splash into the water and pretending that they had let it hit the seabed. Hence the expression.

Taking "soundings," or using the lead, means simply that while the ship is sailing along a weighted line with depth marks on it is heaved ahead of the ship and allowed to sink until it hits the bottom. Just as it becomes vertical—as the ship sails forward —the leadsman reads the depth mark and yells out "By the mark five" (or whatever it might be). He keeps this up as long as the vessel is in water shallow enough for the skipper to be concerned about running aground.

In small yachts soundings are not often taken in this way in water deeper than five fathoms (thirty feet), and the marks are unlikely to be the traditional ones of leather, canvas, bunting, etc. A simple system of one knot for one fathom, two knots for two fathoms, etc., is much more usual. However, the method of swinging the lead must be learned because it is one of those jobs which a woman can take over.

First of all, don't fall overboard. Most of the time both hands will be needed for the lead and this is always a bit dangerous if the ship is rolling. Make sure the end of the line is made fast on board, otherwise you could lose it overboard if the lead weight should stick in a muddy bottom. Coil the line and divide it just as for the heaving line. Hold the throwing part with the lead just clear of the surface of the water, then swing it forward, backward and then forward again with force and let it go when it is just a bit higher than the horizontal, aiming it to drop into the water alongside the bow. The line will whistle out as the lead sinks, and after a bit of practice it is easy to feel when it hits the bottom. When it does, the slack must be gathered in quickly so that when it is alongside (as the ship sails forward) the line is straight up and down with no slackness. A glance at the water surface to read the mark, or guess how much under or over the nearest mark it is, tells the depth of water, which must be relayed to the skipper as quickly as possible. Remember your back will probably be to the man at the helm so it won't be easy for him to hear you, especially over noises of wind and sea.

Nowadays a good many small sailboats have echo-sounders which do all the work, but it is a good idea to know how to take a leadline sounding—electronics can fail. Reading the echo-sounder is very simple, but for the person assigned to it there is still a right and a wrong way to do the job. The skipper will want to know the depths (always assuming that he can't see the instrument) at regular intervals and it is an annoyance to have to keep asking for a reading. Whether the reading alters or not, keep announcing the depths in steady succession—about every five to ten seconds—until told to stop it or to note only alterations. Supposing there had been a steady four fathoms for some time, the skipper would want to be told of any shoaling or deepening, and the steeper the rise or fall the more rapidly the soundings must be read out. Again speak clearly. With any navigational uncertainty prevailing men tend to become a bit edgy for all that they may present a façade of unruffled calm.

Fenders

Fenders are referred to elsewhere in this book, but they are a subject which can be given a fairly thorough treatment because if ever there was a woman's deck job, then handling fenders is certainly it. The whole purpose of a fender, or "fendoff" as it is sometimes called, is to protect the yacht. Whenever she goes alongside anywhere, or anything, fenders are dropped between hull and quay, etc., to take the shocks and the chafe. If the skipper gets himself into a spot and finds that willy-nilly he is about to go alongside something (in other words he is going to *hit* it) a well placed fender produced in time by someone who didn't need to be told can be the salvation of the situation.

Fenders vary from pneumatic ones to plastic cylinders, old motor tires to rope ones (very heavy when wet), but they all do the same job. They all have a length of rope by which they can be secured to the guard rail or to some other strong point so that they hang down outside the hull *at the right height.* It is no good lowering a fender into the water where it will lie under the curve of the hull. Neither is it much use hanging it onto the stern to dangle in mid-air. According to the shape of the yacht and the nature of the thing which she is going to hit (or go alongside) the fender must be positioned where it will be of most value.

This is where your knowledge of knots comes in. It is not sufficient to be able to secure the fender with the right hitch; the hitch must be made and drawn tight so that the fender is in the intended spot. Imagine doing up a parcel tightly with string and then making a slack knot—the same thing.

Usually a clove hitch is suitable, but a round turn and two half-hitches is equally effective. Just in case there is a last minute change of plan, or circumstances make it vital to put the other side of the yacht alongside at the last minute, don't secure all your fenders along one side. Always keep at least one handy and make sure the hitches on the rest can be slipped undone quickly.

The usual position for fenders is at the widest part of the hull, just by or abaft the main rigging. One might be hung well up and halfway to the bows and another one, or possibly two, aft by the cockpit. Finally, never leave fenders lying around unsecured on the cabin top. They can easily roll overboard, so always secure them with a slip knot.

Secure for the night

When a small sailboat comes to anchor for the night, there are a lot of things to be done after she has been securely anchored. Usually this is the point at which the woman goes below, sorts out the chaos and begins to think about supper, but if there is a plan to eat ashore it is a case of all hands to snug down the ship.

The sails must be properly stowed, with headsails bagged and sent to their stowage space. There are various ideas for stowing a mainsail. Some people don't bother much about neatness and simply put a few lashings or stops on, then secure the sail coat over all. A good sail stow is worth doing, though. Not only does it look neat and seaman-like, but the sail is secure should it come on to blow during the night (Fig. 37).

The battens may or may not be taken out. Personally I believe

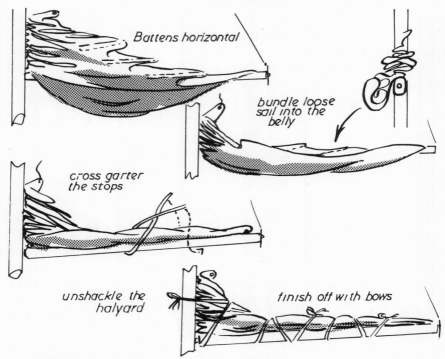

Fig. 37: Stowing a mainsail. If the battens are to be left ready for instant use, the folds of sail must first be gathered so that the battens are horizontal to the boom. The foot of the sail is formed into a bag and the rest of the material is bundled into it. Finally it is rolled tight and secured by stops as shown. It may be necessary to take the top batten out for a really neat stow—otherwise it could get broken

in leaving them in because one never knows when it may be necessary to get under way in the dark—and quickly at that. First the sail, which is still secured to both the boom and the mast, is all pulled over to one side, then the leech (the back edge) is pulled forward on top of the boom and the bottom part of the loose sail is drawn out sideways and held to make a sort of bag into which all the loose sail is tumbled. This can then be rolled up and the stops made fast.

Jib sheets must be secured each side and coiled; so must the mainsheet. There may be a prop, or crutch, into which the boom is lowered; if not, then the topping lift is adjusted so that the boom is "topped up" high enough to clear heads and the boom sheeted down tightly to hold it secure. Halyards are pulled tight and secured by the "gilguys" which pull them away from the mast. These short lines go round the main shrouds and the idea is to stop the halyards tapping against the mast at night. The burgee may be hauled down and the ensign at the stern lowered. There is also the riding light, or anchor light, to hoist. This is a lantern which is hung as high as possible up the forestay as a warning to other craft moving around at night. Some are kerosine-filled, others run from dry or ship's batteries.

The bilges may need pumping after a hard sail, there may be a bow fender to sling (a special type which hangs under the bow like a necklace and keeps the chain away from the hull), and a couple of ordinary fenders may be hung alongside the cockpit for the dinghy to lie alongside.

The dinghy may need bailing out if it has been towed. If it is to be left afloat for the night it may either be moored against those fenders and secured bow and stern, or secured astern on its painter. In the latter case it may be decided to take the deck bucket on its line and make it fast to the stern of the dinghy, allowing the bucket to sink. This cuts down the risk of the dinghy becoming a nuisance in the night if at any time the wind and tide should be in opposition. Being subject to the wind rather than the tide, the dinghy could come ranging up and hit the anchored yacht again and again. The bucket, dragged by the current, reduces the likelihood of this. Finally, the skipper may decide to take the mop and give the decks a last swabbing down before calling it a day.

All in all, quite a lot of work, to say nothing of extra small repairs needed, engine maintenance, and so on. But for all that, I don't know of many things as satisfying as snugging down for the night in some sheltered creek at sunset.

7/A Stage Further

The night watch

There is a great deal more to learn before the man in the case becomes worried about his status as expert. The more you learn the smoother the management of the yacht will be and the happier all concerned. More to the point, the safer everyone becomes, because in a small sailboat, the concentration of all the skills in one person is rather a hazardous arrangement.

While the possibility of an emergency in which the woman has to take over the whole show must always be considered to exist, it is happily a remote exigency; more immediate is the value of a woman who can manage the ship while the skipper gets some rest. Anyone who has sailed offshore knows how difficult it is to sleep unless one has complete confidence in those on deck and their ability to cope with steamer traffic, or handle the yacht in variations of wind strength and direction. Only when a man knows that the woman on deck is fully capable of reacting sensibly to the changing situation and that she is experienced enough to recognize a potential emergency, and will call him, can he rest with an easy mind.

The first night at sea is the greatest adventure. It may also be cold and a bit frightening. The skipper may decide to stay up all night and leave his crew to sail the ship in daylight while he sleeps a little, or he may sleep for an hour or two around midnight if all seems to be well. In normal weather and with a small crew of perhaps a man and wife, a child, and maybe one other adult, the skipper may elect to take the middle of the night (from 11:00 P.M. to 3:00 A.M.), letting the others share the remainder of the dark hours. If the other adult is experienced they might well share the whole night between them, or give the wife the first watch from dusk to 11:00 P.M.; but if the extra adult is inexperienced the wife will be the watch officer and the skipper will rest "on call."

According to the plot, land is somewhere over there. It's nice to be the first to see land on the horizon, but nicer still to find that navigation and steering have been spot-on

Without doubt the most important of all night duties is to watch for steamers. The course must be steered and an eye kept lifted for changes of wind, but the vital matter is to see that the yacht is sailed safely past big shipping.

Around the coasts of every well-populated country the steamers pass in steady succession. They converge at major headlands and in the vicinity of ports and navigable rivers and they follow distinct "lanes" at sea. At the Straits of Dover, for instance, something like seven hundred big ships pass every twenty-four hours. Between these lanes go the smaller vessels such as coasters and in fishing areas there are the trawlers and drifters.

The Rules of the Road at sea state that power-driven vessels nearly always must give way to sailing craft, but this is a law to be looked at with sense. They give way if they can and if they can *see you*. Some try to shave past close without altering their course; others may *appear* to give way, but in fact they are really swerving to and fro due to difficulty in steering which is caused by their being in ballast, or unloaded, and high in the water. Some alter course because they have spotted another big ship, way beyond the small yacht, which they may well not have seen. Years ago, in a big 50=ton schooner, my husband and I were actually run down in this way. Fortunately we were hit a glancing blow, which didn't prove too serious. It turned out that the mail ship, some 14,000 tons, which had altered course four separate times, didn't see us from first to last despite the fact that we made every effort to be seen.

Don't be alarmed by all this. A small yacht is very unlikely to be run down so long as the basic rules are observed. The important thing is to keep a very close watch on any large ship until her lights show that she is safely past, in case she alters course suddenly just when you assumed her to be well clear.

The lights carried by ships must be understood and they are really very simple to grasp. Every powered vessel over 150 feet must carry two white masthead lights in addition to port and starboard side lights and a stern light; the side lights must be visible from ahead to two points (22-1/2 degrees) abaft the beam. This means that the red port light, for instance, cannot be seen from the starboard side, but on the port side it can be seen until she passes from broadside-on to a little ahead of this point. From then on her white stern light becomes visible. The two white masthead lights, one slightly forward and lower than the other, can be seen from all angles until the ship is past the broadside-on position and beginning to go away. When she is past, only her stern light can be seen. (A non-seagoing vessel operating under U.S. Inland Rules may carry a 32=point range light which is visible from every side.)

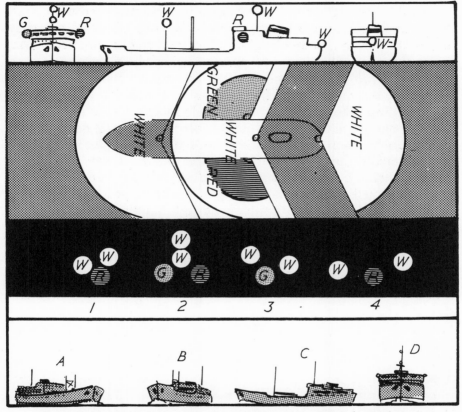

Fig. 38: Lights and shipping. Memorize the positions of lights on this typical steamer and then try to visualize the angle at which the ship is lying from the "lights" shown in the black strip. See if you can match them up with the ships at the bottom. (Answers at end of Chapter)

Thus, by mentally sorting out the lights seen and their relative positions to each other, it is possible to judge whether a ship is passing on a parallel course, moving away, coming head-on or approaching at an angle on a converging course—which may or may not be a collision course! The diagrams include a simple test; have a good look at them and see if you can judge the courses of the ships concerned (Fig. 38).

The distance and speed of big ships is difficult to assess at first. One moment a ship is a distant twinkle of lights, the next they are high up and glowing brightly. The white lights are seen first, then the colored ones, and finally lights from portholes and elsewhere can be seen reflected in the water. By now the ship is getting so close that the yacht should not be on anything approaching a collision course. If in doubt it's a safe plan to call the skipper when the colored lights become visible. If both colored lights can be seen at the same time, but very small and distant, it will mean that, providing you are moving nicely, you have passed ahead, but *watch that ship closely.* If you continue to see both colored lights she is coming straight at you. Always note how wide apart the white masthead lights appear because when they draw close together the ship is heading your way.

There is a simple trick for estimating a collision course (Fig. 39). Steer the yacht as straight as possible and sit quite still. Find some object on the yacht, such as a winch or stay, which is in line with the lights of the converging steamer. Do this when she

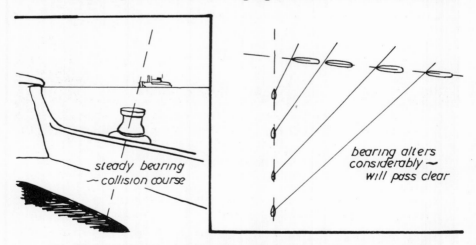

steady bearing — collision course

bearing alters considerably — will pass clear

Fig. 39: Collision course. By keeping the steamer in line with some part of the yacht while steering a dead straight course and sitting still, it can be seen whether the steamer will pass clear or whether the two craft are on a collision course

is still a very long way off. If it is a collision course, and you keep your head still, then the ship, the object and your eye will remain in line as the two vessels draw closer; but if they come out of line, and you are certain your course has been straight, it is fairly safe to assume that all is well. But *watch her.* This trick doesn't work so well if you are both approaching at a narrow angle or in rough conditions.

Obviously there's no need to take a bearing by hand bearing compass with land around like this, but this is the ideal time to practice taking bearings and plotting them on the chart. Once the sea wife starts taking an interest in the real seamanship and navigation she opens up a whole new interest for herself as well as adding to the strength and know-how of the crew

Never be slow to call the skipper, even if he is very tired and has just gone to sleep. I have called my husband time and again. He has gritted his teeth when the reason has turned out to be trivial, but he has never said anything because he relies on me to do just this.

Rules of the Road at sea

Anyone in charge of a boat at sea should know the Rules of the Road—the highway code of the sea. Just as important, anyone who is likely to be left at the helm should have an understanding of the basic rules at least. Situations can develop quickly. Another vessel, hitherto passing safely, may suddenly alter course, and a split-second decision to avoid collision may be vital. Briefly, here are the important points to watch.

Big ships must always be regarded seriously. The old basic rule "power gives way to sail" still holds good, but don't try to enforce it! Never pass close ahead of a steamer although it may be your right technically. You can never be 100 percent certain that you have been seen. In fact never rely upon being seen in the open sea at night. Keep clear of big shipping in channels and restricted waters; sudden and violent course changes may be necessary as the ship maneuvers to follow a narrow channel, so give plenty of sea room.

Under sail the starboard tack boat has precedence whether running (boom out to port), reaching or close-hauled under International Rules, but under U.S. Inland Rules a close-haul boat has the right-of-way over a boat that is running free. When two sailing boats have the wind on the same side, the vessel which is to windward must keep clear. The overtaking vessel, on any point of sailing, must keep clear of those it overtakes. Racing yachts (those flying the square burgee) sail to a more complicated set of rules and to avoid spoiling their sport other sailing vessels usually give them right of way. However, it is worth noting that this is a courtesy gesture only—although taken for granted by the majority of racing skippers—and when it comes to the law only the international rules for preventing collisions apply on high seas. Inland waters of the United States are presently controlled by U.S. Inland Rules of the Road except for special rules on the Great Lakes and western rivers. The basic principles of all rules are quite similar, however.

In channels, keep to the starboard side when approaching another vessel head-on; but don't cut across his bows in order to get to the starboard side; if you are passing safely, hold your course. Consider whether there is a bend in the channel and whether the other ship (if large) is likely to make an alteration of course which will conflict with yours.

If the engine is on (whether the sails are set or not) the boat is classed as a powered vessel and, in most cases, must give way to ALL craft under sail. A vessel under power gives way to other power vessels approaching and converging from the starboard side unless that vessel is the overtaking one. Once again it is up to the overtaking vessel to keep clear of those it overtakes. When approaching head-on at sea, turn to starboard a little to pass port-to-port.

Big ships blow their sirens to signal their intentions to turn. One blast means, "I am altering my course to starboard," two blasts, "I am altering my course to port," and three blasts, "My engines are going astern." If a ship on the high seas blows five short blasts, beware, she may be saying "You are in danger of colliding with me." Four short blasts can signify danger under the U.S. Inland Rules.

The tides

Whole books are written about the behavior of the tides and it is a truly vast subject. I must, therefore, leave out the technical stuff and deal with the sort of tidal knowledge which I, as a sailing wife, have assimilated.

Obedient to the pull of sun and moon, the surface of the world's seas and oceans is lifted and, as the earth spins, a very shallow tidal wave runs around the globe. In shallow waters and in confined waters, such as the English Channel, the tidal wave is made to build up into a bigger concentration of water. An extreme case is the Bristol Channel where the funnel effect of the narrowing river causes a tidal "bore" which actually becomes a wall of water several feet high as the tide builds up. All this means is that some places have a low rise and fall of tide while others have a much bigger one.

The tide doesn't reach the highest level at every time of high water. Week and week after we get neap tides—which are lower ones—and spring tides which rise higher; this is due to the amount of pull exerted by the sun and moon when working either together or against each other. Several times each year come the really big tides and the equinoctial periods. We get two high waters in each 24 hours, but because the cycles of low water to high water and back to low water occupy a bit more than 12 hours, the times of high water are just a bit later each day. For example it might be high water at 8:00 A.M. today in a certain place, but tomorrow it would be high water at, say, 8:50 A.M., and so on.

Because the tidal current floods along the coasts and up the rivers and then ebbs back again, the times of high water vary from port to port all over the world. In England, to save having hundreds of tide tables, we have everything based on "HW Dover" in home waters and add or subtract a bit to find the high-water times for other places. Other countries do likewise. The Atlantic coast of North America, for instance, has twenty-one reference stations or tidal current predictions.

There is one other thing about tidal rise and fall which is important. The water level doesn't creep up and down at the same speed. After low water it begins to rise slowly at first, then quicker and quicker until the middle of the rise, after which the rate of rise slows down again. The same thing happens in reverse on the ebb.

To "catch a tide," therefore, is to be at the right place when the current is beginning to go the way you want to go, and to have a "foul" tide is to have it against you. It can also catch you sideways and set you off course unless a course is planned which allows for this.

There is one hoary old misconception which even trips up people who should know better; novelists in droves fall for it. If someone said that a yacht was becalmed and not moving and the boathook which fell overboard was *taken out of reach by the tide,* they would be talking nonsense. Unless the yacht was anchored, both it and the boathook would be moving together on the tide.

It is like sitting in a chair in the middle of a carpet which is slowly being towed along. A dropped book would lie by your chair where it fell despite the fact that both you and the book were being towed along.

How does a sea wife fit into all this? Being aware of the importance of tides makes her more willing to shape her shopping plans to suit the situation. She will understand why the engine may have to be started at sea sometimes and why it is so rarely possible to arrive when you expected to arrive. Also why departures are sometimes made at unearthly hours, why anchorages are sometimes far from the landing place, and why the sea suddenly becomes rough: wind blowing against the current does this.

In addition to understanding the tides she can use her knowledge to good effect. If shopping has to be done and she takes the dinghy, she must know where to leave it. She must know what the tide is doing when she goes ashore and what it is likely to

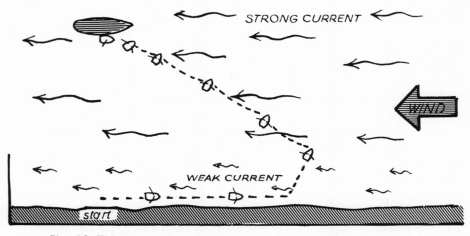

Fig. 40: This rower, faced with a strong crosswind and current, is going about things the sensible way. She has rowed well upstream close to the shore, where the current is generally weaker, and in due course she cuts across, rowing crab-wise, finally rowing head to current and wind and allowing them to drop her down to the moored craft. Note that she goes alongside well towards the bow

be doing when she is ready to return. This might mean pulling
a dinghy well up a slipway before securing the painter, otherwise
a flooding tide could put it out of reach later on. She might time
her row ashore so that the current is with her each way. Likewise
she might row carefully along the shallow edges of the shore or
river banks where the current is slackest, to avoid a hard pull,
and on her return shortly afterwards, row bang down the middle
in deep water so that she has the full benefit of the current. This
is practical tidal lore (Fig. 40).

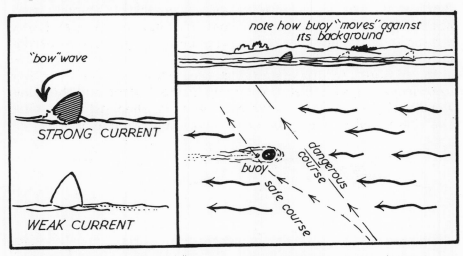

Fig. 41: In a fast tidal current moored craft and buoys must be
watched closely. Note the bow wave around the one shown top left.
Note also when sailing with the current fair how quickly moored
objects seem to move along the shore background—this is a good
guide to the speed of the current. When the current is against you
(a foul tide), the objects may seem to stand still or move the wrong
way if no progress is being made against the current. Always steer
to pass downstream of any moored objects on your course

At sea, when she has the tiller, the sea wife will mentally
review the tidal situation when passing big navigational buoys
(Fig. 41). When one is sailing across the current a buoy must be
passed *down-current* unless it can be passed well up-current,

otherwise the yacht may be swept on to it and possibly suffer serious damage. Anything anchored or moored or sticking up from the seabed must be watched with caution in a tideway—other vessels which are *not* moored will be moving on the same tidal stream (the carpet).

The relation of tidal rise and fall to the figures of depth shown on the chart is a complicated business and well worth learning in due course. For our purpose, though, we will be content to generalize. When passing a buoy which can be identified on the chart, a reading on the echo-sounder (or a leadline sounding) makes it possible to compare the depth found with the depth shown for that position on the chart. This is usually deeper than the chart says, since those charted depths show what amounts to the level at very low, low tides.

By looking up the time of high water for the area it will be possible to see whether it is high water, low water, or at some stage in between. We have seen that there is (probably) more water under us than the chart shows at that spot. Now we can tell whether to expect still more depth (tide is flooding) or whether the level is going to fall until it becomes more like the figures given on the chart (tide is ebbing). All this touches on whether it is safe to carry on into shallower water or whether the yacht should head for deeper water.

Suppose now that we anchor our yacht in some creek. It is high tide and we must know whether we will stay afloat at low tide. The tide tables may show that this particular tide has a height of 12 feet; there is only 15 feet of water and our yacht needs 3 feet to float in. It might seem that we are exactly right and that her keel will just touch at low tide. This is the tricky bit. That height of 12 feet means that the tide will rise 12 feet above the figures shown on the chart, known as Chart Datum. Unfortunately the level doesn't always fall to the chart figure. If you have a tide table which gives the height of *low tide* as well as high tide (U. S. Coast and Geodetic Survey Tide Table), it's easy. All that has to be done is subtract the low water height from the high water height.

The result is called the "range" and this is the distance that the level ranges up and down from low water to high water. Thus, if we found in this case that the range turned out to be 9 feet we'd know that, since it is high tide, the level will fall 9 feet and that low water level will be 9 feet from 15 feet, leaves 6 feet—in other words, there will be a good 6 feet of water at low tide. There are ways of finding the range if the tide tables are not on hand, but enough's enough for the time being.

We must know what the range is if we are to be able to calculate how much the level will rise or fall above the low tide mark. Likewise we don't always anchor conveniently at high tide. It may

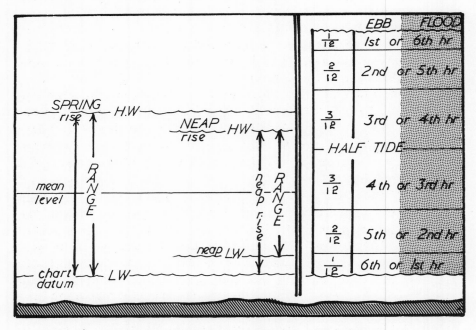

Fig. 42: How the tides work. The mean spring rise is roughly equal to the extent that it "ranges" up and down between low and high water. Neap tides neither rise as high nor fall as low, consequently they range up and down a shorter distance. The table on the right shows the "twelfths" rule. The period is not quite a convenient 6 hours, but about 6 hours 12.5 minutes on average

be one-half flood or three-quarters ebb. Easiest of all is when we anchor at dead low tide because we can see at once whether there is enough water to float in—if there isn't, we go aground.

There is a very simple rule for working out the amount of tide that will rise, or fall, above low water (Fig. 42). We have seen how the level moves quickest around half tide either flood or ebb. Now, in the first hour of ebb or flood the level moves roughly one-twelfth of the total range. It moves two-twelfths in the second hour, then three-twelfths in the third, three-twelfths in the fourth, two-twelfths in the fifth and one-twelfth in the final or sixth hour (six hours roughly from low water to high water). To be even rougher in our calculations we can say that the level rises to, or falls to, a quarter in the first two hours, half in three hours, and three-quarters in the fourth hour. You may never have to choose an anchorage, but at least you will understand why the skipper may mess about and make supper late.

Reading the chart

The main difference between a map and a chart is that whereas a map concentrates detail upon features of the land, the chart is concerned with coast and seabed—which is why only idiots attempt to use maps for navigation. Reading a chart consists of being able to look at the land and then look at the chart and reconcile the one with the other. It also means that you can study the chart when the land is out of sight and, assuming that you know your whereabouts, visualize where you are going on the chart, how long you are going to take to get there, and what the seabed beneath you is like. You will know where to look on the horizon when land is expected, which lights and lighthouses you may expect to see, and so on. The important thing is to always have a "feeling" of position on the chart as well as having a plotted position. This means that as you sit steering you will feel that land is just over *that* horizon in *that* direction and know at what angle the yacht is sailing relative to coast, lightships, shipping lanes, and so on.

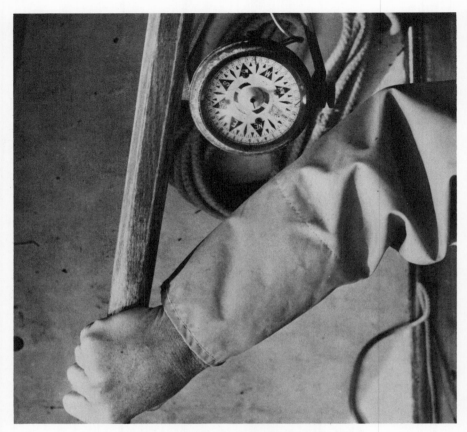

A steering compass mounted below the tiller

When the coast is in sight, you will be able to glance at the chart and then at the land and say: "Ah, that misty line must be this headland just coming into view. . ." From this sort of chart reading you will then be able to look around and search for the buoys, prominent church towers, and so on, which the chart tells you you should be able to see. In a small yacht the horizon is only just over three miles away at that low eye level, and low objects will not be visible until they have lifted clear of the horizon, but the chart tells you in which direction to stare.

Every chart has a compass rose on it which also shows "magnetic" north. This is roughly the same north direction as the steering compass shows and while I don't propose to go into detail here (and it is an involved business) it is sufficient to remember that if you are steering west, for instance, and you note where the magnetic west on the chart is aimed, the yacht will be headed in that direction from wherever she happens to be on the chart.

Not every steering compass is accurate. Metalwork in the boat and other influences drag the magnet of the compass out of proper alignment and this "deviation" must be allowed for. This is the skipper's job, but it will explain why the course to steer may differ from that drawn on the chart. For *approximate* courses and bearings and assuming that the chart is a recent one (because magnetic north changes gradually over the years), it is possible to say that any course line drawn on the chart and then read off by transferring it to the magnetic part of the rose with the parallel rules, can be steered by yacht's compass. This is such a generalization as to be heretical, and the result might be so inaccurate that your eventual landfall could be well off, but, lacking a fuller knowledge of navigation, a rough heading taken this way would at least allow you to navigate *towards* help if some misfortune left you in charge of the ship. Ideally, a regular crew member should set about learning simple navigation in greater detail.

The chart is a mass of information. The symbols show rocks, wrecks, buoys of different sorts, depths, shoals, deep channels, and so on. Many are self-explanatory, others less obvious. Each chart, like a map, is drawn to a particular scale as well. You must know the scale before you can go much further. In terms of nautical miles (longer than land miles) you have only to look at the scale drawn on the *sides* of the sheet. This is Latitude. One minute of latitude is one nautical mile. The scale at the top and the bottom of the chart is the Longitude and must not be used for measuring distance in miles.

The other vital thing to check is whether the figures showing

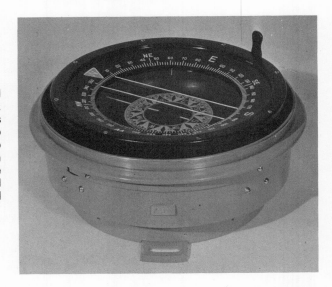

A typical yacht grid steering compass. The course chosen is set by turning the top ring so that the two bars are aligned with it. To steer the course the line on the card must be kept parallel with the grid pair

depths mean feet or fathoms. Soon all charts may be metric, but depths in any mathematical language are important. It might be that figures relate to fathoms in deep water, fathoms and feet in shallower water, and feet where the seabed dries out at low tide. In the last case any figure having a line drawn under it means soundings or reefs that uncover.

Make a habit of looking at the chart whenever you think of it. If a buoy is in sight, find it on the chart and then consider where the yacht is in relation to it. Suppose the buoy is about a mile away on your port bow, about halfway between the bow and the broadside-on position. Look for the buoy on the chart, then look at the course you are sailing and picture an imaginary boat at the position which would allow it to have the buoy on a line between bow and beam (that broadside-on position). What you have done in effect is to take a bearing by eye.

If two buoys are visible, one beyond the other, and they come into line with each other you have only to draw a line on the chart through these buoys to know that the yacht must be somewhere on that line. This is a "transit," or line of position. If a buoy was absolutely dead ahead of the yacht and you glanced at the course she was steering, you would have taken a compass or "magnetic bearing" of the buoy—allowing for deviation of the compass being conveniently nil, of course.

These three sorts of navigational checks are the basis of coastwise pilotage. Buoys, churches, headlands, lightships, and so on are identified on the chart and then used in one way or other as you sail along, and each contributes a little bit more to establishing exactly where you are on the chart. Combine this with study of the depth, allowance for tidal currents, and the plotting of a course line from what you are actually able to steer according to where the wind is, and you have a good overall conception of what it is all about. You will soon take it a step further and begin using the hand bearing compass to take your own bearings.

This instrument is simply a little compass with a prism sight on it which is lined up with some object, after which the bearing shown in the prism is read off. There is a knack to using the compass in anything of a seaway and it is worth practicing. Having read off a bearing, say 170 degrees, you then go to the chart, find the object of your bearing, and then lay the rules across the middle of the magnetic rose with the edge on 170. "Walking" the rules across the chart until the edge is on the object and drawing a pencil line tell you that the yacht is somewhere on that line. Now, if you can find another identifiable object at roughly right angles to the first and take another bearing and plot it, the crossing of the pencil lines will be, in theory, where you are on the chart. Again there are small adjustments to be made to these bearings for complete accuracy. If it is possible to take a third object between the first two and repeat the process, there will be an intersection of pencil lines in the form of a small triangle—a "cocked hat." The yacht will be somewhere in the middle of it. The smallness of this hat is the measure of your care in taking the bearings and the accuracy of your compass (Fig. 43).

From all this it can be seen how important it is to steer the best compass course possible; and if you have not been able to keep dead on course to be able to tell the navigator your *average* course and what you think your error has been during the time you have been steering. A sensible skipper makes a point of being nice about it if the helmsman admits candidly that the course hasn't been dead on. If he is nasty he has only himself to blame if he plots one course on the chart while the ship, due to the helmsman's reluctance to own up, has been steering a bit adrift.

Steering by compass is a knack soon mastered, but it takes more

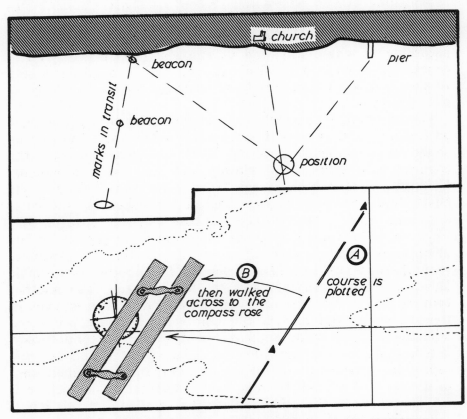

Fig. 43: Bearings and courses. Shown here are a three-point fix by compass and a position line obtained by having two identifiable marks in line. The bottom sketch shows how a plotted course is transferred by means of the parallel rules to the nearest compass rose on the chart so that its magnetic (or true) bearing can be read

than a knack to become a good helmsman. Too much tiller-waving makes the yacht go slower. The aim is to sense each off-course swing and anticipate it by a gentle pressure of the tiller one way or the other.

The compass may be a conventional type with a card marked in degrees and a heavy black or white line (the "lubber line") on the side of the compass bowl. When the course required is in line with the lubber line, the ship is on course and the card will be moving from side to side as the ship swerves. The good helmsman sees to it that the card swings an equal amount each way, thus steering a correct average course. In flat seas the card may be easy to hold on the line for long spells, but at other times it seeks to swing wildly and tends to swing more one way than the other.

The first thing to remember is that the card is, theoretically, stationary and that the yacht is swinging around it since the card magnet is constantly pointing its north end towards the earth's magnetic field. By studying the movement of the tiller and the movement of the lubber line you will be able to imagine that you are pushing or pulling the line back and forth.

Another popular type of compass is the grid. This has a "T" on the card and another "T" on the glass top of the bowl. The navigator sets the course he wants by turning the grid glass and the helmsman thereafter tries to keep the two "T's" in line with each other. Wherever the helmsman may be sitting at the tiller the grid remains easy to use because there is always some part of the system which can be lined up with the card.

This is a bare taste of what navigation is about. Many women take to navigation at once and become very good at it. For the time being it is enough just to understand the rudiments of the subject.

(Answer to steamer light test in Fig. 38: 1–B, 2–D, 3–A and 4–C.)

8/Coping with Emergencies

Whether you are living adventurously or just sitting at home, emergencies of one sort or another seem to arise, and sailing is no different from anything else. The prudent, careful yachtsman gets into very little trouble, but the threat still exists and in point of fact trouble often arises through no fault of your own. Nearly all emergencies, casualties, and lifeboat rescues could have been avoided if the people concerned had known how to cope with the first scent of trouble.

Fire

Such things as a pan of hot fat getting alight, a kerosine lamp being knocked over, meths spilling and catching fire, an engine fault, inadequate asbestos protection for a heating stove or a cooker, etc., more often than not are the causes of fires on yachts. More dangerous are explosions caused by gasoline spillage, back-fire, bottled gas leakage, etc. Explosions must be regarded with absolute dread. An egg-cup full of gasoline, mixing with air at the critical temperature, is the equivalent of a stick of TNT —and so is a bilge full of escaped cooking gas. A woman in a small yacht can, and should, be the ship's conscience. If her man is careless with gasoline, she should protest in the strongest terms. The gas bottle is her charge and she should think of it as a bomb—which is however completely harmless providing she and her family observe the rules.

The first essential with fire, afloat as ashore, is to keep your head. Small fires are usually easy to deal with by smothering them with a cloth, but they are dangerous if they occur close to a gasoline engine or a gas bottle or anything else of an inflammable nature. It may not be necessary to spray the whole accommodation with a fire extinguisher, but an extinguisher should be ready at hand and known to be in working condition.

There are many different types of fire extinguishers on the market and I won't go into detail here except to say that a recommended type should be chosen and that it should not be one of those tiny aerosols. These are all right as a galley stand-by,

This stove is situated just inside the companionway, which means that the fire extinguisher can be grabbed from the cockpit if necessary

but at least two extinguishers, pint-size or quart-size, should be ready at hand, in clips on the paneling—although not right above the stove! (In the United States fire extinguishers must meet certain legal requirements. You can consult the Coast Guard regulations or the Motor Boat Act for the type and number of fire extinguishers required.)

If a fire breaks out and it seems ominous, order everybody out on deck right away, but don't open the forehatch or do anything to increase the draft. Tell someone to turn off the gas bottle or do it yourself. If the skipper knows his job he will turn the ship so that any flames are blown away from the cockpit where people will be gathered and where the fuel tanks may be situated. If the fire looks bad, get the dinghy ready, see that there are lifejackets available and that someone has charge of the distress rockets.

These are the basic precautions and may have to be applied according to the situation, but the essentials are calm, readiness, the habit of looking ahead. The skipper should be the one to take charge and only one person can be in command, but a useful crew can save the day by doing the right things without having to be told. Above all, don't allow such a situation to develop in the first place. A cigarette could start a fire, or the hot ashes from a pipe.

Provide deep, heavy, uncapsizeable ashtrays and take similar precautions with all those fire-raising possibilities.

Man overboard

This is a sneaky and dreadful danger, but it need never arise. There is always a *reason* for someone falling overboard; strictly speaking it is not an "accident." Carelessness, over-familiarity, and failure to observe sensible precautions are the causes. It is possible to be washed overboard in heavy weather of the worst

This lifebuoy on a long line is ideal for throwing to anyone in the water so long as the yacht is traveling at slow speed. If she is traveling fast it could be wrenched out of grasp. This fitting, called the Quoit., can be screwed or glued down on deck ready for use in emergency

sort, but not *lost* overboard providing sensible seamanlike precautions have been taken.

Lifelines, lifejackets, and safety harnesses are the main safety factors, plus care at all times. Forget the idea that danger only exists in heavy weather; this is simply not true. It *always* exists. Nobody advocates wearing lifejackets or flotation garments night and day in calm, serene weather, nor is it necessary to wear safety harnesses; but at these times, and especially at night, one takes special care not to be lulled into a sense of false security.

The outstanding risks occur in unguarded moments. A plastic "draw" bucket being emptied may tempt someone to use both hands at once in order to make it drop into the water upside down. A man might balance for a moment while taking a sounding with the leadline, or he might forget to hang on in the excitement of the moment. Always hook an arm round a stay, for instance, when using two hands to take a bearing or to look through the binoculars.

The action of climbing from cockpit to deck to go forward is a critical one—a lurch could send you over. When the yacht is heeling steeply and you are changing places in the cockpit is another danger moment. In fact more people are lost overboard from the cockpit than from the foredeck.

Children should always wear lifejackets and/or safety harnesses. They will want to move around and to climb because this is their nature, and a pair of stout wires secured along the deck full length provides an anchorage for harness hooks which allows them to roam safely in fine weather.

It should be remembered that a lifejacket in the true meaning of the word is so designed that it will float an unconscious person face upwards. A "swimming aid" may be a buoyant garment, a waistcoat or any one of many similar designs. (The differences are outlined fully in Chapter 12, Children Afloat.) The swimming aid will support a person in the water, but it will not necessarily float him face upwards. The crux of the matter is that while the lifejacket is usually bulky and tends to restrict movement the swimming aid restricts movement hardly at all. One may fall overboard without warning. Is it better to wear a swimming aid at all times when a risk exists and be unimpeded by it, or to wear a lifejacket and perhaps be restricted in one's movements? The important thing is that some sort of buoyant aid should not only be on board for each person, but that it should be at hand always and frequently worn.

It is the skipper usually who decides when buoyancy should be worn. At night, in the dinghy, in choppy weather or in bad conditions at sea he might order "jackets on." He will probably make it a rule in fog, when there is shipping about, and in any other emergency, or simply as a precaution for a non-swimmer.

It is better not to fall overboard in the first place, and the safety harness is designed with this in mind. If there is a reluctance to wear both harness and jacket (and on top of oilskins and sweaters this all adds up to an untidy, restrictive bundle), the harness is first choice at night and in rough weather, or at any time when finding and picking up a person is likely to be difficult. Buoyant jackets can be obtained that are light weight, warm, waterproof, and non-bulky. These might be ideal on a cold night when worn with harnesses. More important than anything is to see that the harness is always hooked on to the ship, and the only exception to this rule is if there is any chance of the yacht sinking or being sunk—in fog among steamers, say. The hook rope may be ten feet long with a midway second hook. Never use the full length unless it is needed as scope for working on deck. Hook up short and stay hooked up. If you want to move, unhook and hook on again at once.

A man overboard at night is in a grave situation and for this reason every yacht liable to be out at night should have a lifebuoy with an automatic light and whistle attached. There should also be a spare lifebuoy and a throwing line. Seeing a man in the water is the all-important thing and a woman may be posted as spotter in the event of such an emergency. She must never take her eyes off him, and it is not easy. The skipper will be turning the yacht in a tricky maneuver and a head among the waves is easily lost even by day.

I won't dwell at length on the pros and cons of different pick-up drills. Instead I will approach the subject from the viewpoint of the woman who, God forbid, may be left at the helm to do the best she can for her skipper in the water. We must assume that

Reefing a sail is not an emergency maneuver, but a reef in time is a great safety factor. When rolling down a reef, the handle rotates the boom like a roller blind and the sail is thus made smaller. The sail will have to be smoothed out along the boom at intervals and the slides will have to be released from the mast track as the sail is wound down. Avoid folds and wrinkles as these stretch a sail out of shape

she can sail the boat by now; not very expertly perhaps, but well enough for simple maneuvers.

First she must get a lifebuoy into the skipper's hands so that he can stay afloat. She may do this by sailing the boat back to him and dropping it as she sails by. Wild throws are a waste of time and in any case the wind could well blow a buoy out of reach before it can be grabbed. She must post her lookout, keep her head and try to do one of several things. She may try the expert's approach of getting down-wind of the man and then luffing head to wind so that the boat shakes the wind out of her sails and stops just alongside him. Unless she is confident of bringing this off it is best not attempted. An easier method is to sail back to him on any course, except one which is before the wind (unlikely in any case), and as she draws near, ease out all the sails to slow the boat until she is close enough to throw a line to him. She must let the sails go completely and leave the boat to look after herself while she helps the man in the water to pull himself alongside. This second method is not foolproof. Under certain conditions the boat will stop, go astern, bear away, sail a little, then stop again, and so on, and the man in the water will be dragged along with her.

She might also, if she knew how, hastily lower the sails, start the engine and motor back to him indifferent to wind and sailing. There are two huge dangers. Hastily lowered sails may mean ropes over the side and the possibility of a rope getting round the propeller. This would put the yacht out of action and allow it to drift further and further away from the man in the water. The other danger is the spinning propeller, which could inflict dreadful injuries. It must be a hard and fast rule that the engine (not just the propeller) is stopped when going alongside anyone in the water. A merely declutched engine may still leave "propeller creep."

Whatever the method used, or attempted, a situation of this sort is serious enough to warrant firing off a distress flare.

The most difficult part of the whole operation is still to come. Unless a yacht has a proper boarding ladder, or bathing ladder, to hang over the side, it is virtually impossible for a woman to haul an exhausted man out of the water. A loop of rope secured each end and hung overboard into the water will help, if she can find time to rig it.

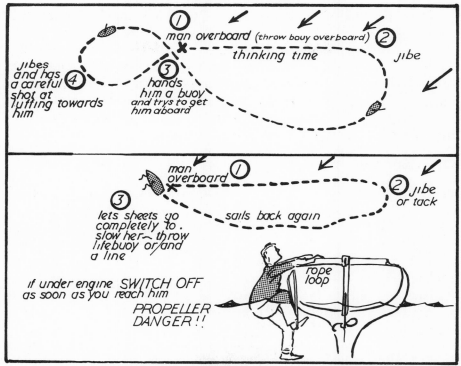

Fig. 44: Man overboard. This maneuver is not the usual one suggested; it is modified to suit the less expert helmsman. The aim is to get a lifebuoy into the swimmer's hands first, thus giving the helmsman a little more time in which to think and act. Arrows represent wind direction. The second example is an operation which the very inexpert might attempt. If she can get the boat back close to the man in the water, lying across the wind, and let the sails flap completely to slow the yacht, she might then get a line to him. Note the propeller warning and the use of a bight or loop as a foot stirrup—very important points

People struggling to climb aboard tire rapidly and it is vital, if such difficulty exists, to pass a rope under the shoulders. This must be secured to the yacht and it means that the body in the water is at least held secure to the yacht if all efforts to get him on board fail and that he will be safe at least, although very uncomfortable until help, summoned by the distress flare, is on hand. Remember the golden rules. Don't lose sight of him, put a lifebuoy into his hands, somehow, and *think* (Fig. 44).

All of which makes depressing reading—but then so do warnings about road accidents and there are fewer dangers at sea than there are ashore. What matters is being able to recognize dangers before they arise. It also becomes apparent how important it is to learn to sail and to master all the other little arts which I advocate in this book.

Distress signals

Distress rockets and flares have been referred to in preceding pages and it is as well to know a little about them. Some years ago in a Skaw Race in the Kattegat a small yacht began to sink in heavy weather and without warning. A very rare occurrence. The distress flares were in a rack just inside the companionway from the cockpit. As the yacht sank under him one of the crew had wit enough to make a grab for them. Actually in the water he fired them off and a yacht, not too far away, saw the red lights and was able to rescue the four-man crew.

We are not ocean racing, but the moral is plain. Have the flares handy, know where they are and how to use them (and without having to read the printed instructions), and make sure everyone else knows too. In the darkness and in a hurry it is too late to start hunting for a flashlight to read labels. Read them at leisure and get to know what the flares feel like in the darkness, too. (The North American Yacht Racing Union safety equipment lists for racing yachts are valuable for any yacht whether she is racing or not.)

Distress signals include red flares and hand-held rockets of various types, and every seagoing yacht should have at least six flares and perhaps two rockets as a minimum. Due to the curvature of the earth a flare will not be visible from a low shore if the yacht is even five miles out to sea; the glow might be seen, but in rainy weather this is by no means certain. A rocket goes up for 200 feet or so and can be seen for many miles, providing there is no very low cloud.

Having attracted attention you then fire the red flares at intervals of, say, five minutes for the first three and at longer intervals for the remainder. One flare, at least, should always be kept as an answering signal should a search vessel begin flashing; otherwise the yacht in distress might not be easily found. A powerful flashlight should also be held ready.

Distress signals cannot be kept forever. They should be renewed according to instructions from the makers and it is a good plan to let off old ones on bonfire night so that all the family can see how they work. (Don't do this if you live by the seashore, though, as the rescue services may turn out!)

Lacking any proper means of summoning assistance it is universally recognized that both arms raised together from the sides to above the head and lowered repeatedly means that help is needed. It may not be possible to stand without holding on with one hand, so any frantic waving of a garment, flag, etc., is the next best thing.

Alternatively any signs of disorder or abnormality can be resorted to. Sails thrown over the side, rigging awry, garments hoisted aloft, sails lowered to flap continually (while you wave) all signify that something is amiss.

If the yacht is under way, a wildly steered course, together with the waving of a white sheet or cloth might do the trick. The traditional signal, the ensign hoisted and flown upside down, is useless since a yacht's ensign is too small to be noticed. Recognized distress signals are given under the various Rules of the Road.

9/The Boatwoman

Handling the dinghy, rowing

Earlier in the book we described the method of getting into and out of a dinghy without disgrace; now it is time to go into boatwork a bit more thoroughly.

The only way to learn to row is to get into a dinghy and do it. A quiet morning when the tide is slack and there is nobody watching is the ideal time. Don't let your husband teach you; just get into the boat, stretch your legs right out and if possible hook your toes under a seat or anything else. This is important. At first you will catch crabs and without the toe-hold go flat on your back. Just sit there, hold the oars so that the blades are upright, dip them into the water and give a very gentle pull. Do no more than this at first and don't try for a full stroke yet. Dip, pull, swing back again, dip, pull, and note your progress. Then pull on one oar alone, then on the other, then both together again —gently. Personally, like a great many other people, I took my first rowing steps in a boating pool and this has a lot to recommend it.

However, boating pools apart, approached in this fashion you will be rowing soon enough and learning to steer by varying the pull on each oar. Keep looking over your shoulder to note progress, but also keep the stern of the boat lined up with some object astern as a guide to whether you are going straight. As confidence grows put more beef into the stroke and swing the oar blades well back for a longer stroke.

When rowing on the sea or when there are wavelets, the oar blades must be lifted high enough to clear the crests, but don't windmill them. Likewise don't dig the blades too deep or you will miss a stroke and go flat on your back—if your feet are not braced.

122

Half the blade's depth is enough. In time, too, you will learn to feather the blades, turning them flat or horizontal for the back-swing in order to reduce windage and inadvertent splashing. With a strong headwind and sea this is important.

In anything of a sea a regular rhythm will not be possible. You must turn your head around and watch the waves as you row into them, timing your stroke so that your pull comes each time a wave rises up. In a beam sea and a following sea this same attention to the waves is needed.

The first crucial test, though, will be to get back alongside the yacht without ramming it head-on. Note first whether the yacht is lying head to current, stern to it (only in a strong wind from the opposite direction), or across the current. If she is lying head to the stream approach in the same way. Row in towards her at an angle, aiming for a point just forward of the cockpit, then at the last moment—a dinghy length away—lift the inside oar out of its oarlock and hold the outside oar in the water so that it both brakes and turns the dinghy. In theory you will slide neatly alongside. According to wind, tide, sea and the strengths of all these forces your approaches will have to be varied, but this is where practice comes into it. Be sure to ship your inboard oarlock so as not to mar the yacht's topsides.

Helping with the fit-out

Nowadays most people do their own maintenance work to save high bills from the local yard, and in any case with fiber glass yachts there isn't so very much of it to do. The bulk of all fitting-out work, be the boat a wood or a glass one, is painting and varnishing, and the preparation for both.

Most men fancy themselves experts at this and most women are relegated to the role of laborer. If a woman can learn what to do, so much the better for her and for the task itself. My husband freely admits that I'm better with the paint brush than he is, but perhaps he's just crafty!

Paints and varnishes are expensive and without proper care and preparation they are wasted. Without going deeply into the techniques of using the various modern finishes let us take a look at the initial stages of the operation. As it gets old, paint becomes scratched, crazed, and faded. In places it may blister, which is usually a sign that it was applied to a wet surface in the first place. Applying new paint to a loose and damaged surface is obviously wrong. If the old paint is very bad it may have to be stripped down to bare wood, either by means of a blowtorch and scraper or by applying paint remover, which is a long and costly job on the whole hull. Both methods are harmful to a fiber glass hull which has been painted. However, today there are paint removers that are harmless to fiber glass.

Having cleaned off a wooden hull, the bare wood must be primed with a special wood primer, undercoated, and the cracks, dents and scratches filled with filler and rubbed down flat again. Then the final paint is applied coat after coat, each being rubbed down with progressively finer abrasive paper until the final coat can be applied. This is a very bald description of the process.

The use of a scraper is the first technique. Unless it is correctly used it will cause more damage than no scraping at all. There is a "grain" to all timber. You brush your hair "with the grain" so to speak and if you brushed it against the grain it would all stand on end. Wood is the same; if you scrape against the grain you produce a jagged, rough surface. Where timber bends in a curve a similar rule applies; scrape with the curve, not against it.

If you can sharpen your own scraper, so much the better; there's nothing worse than trying to manage with a blunt scraper because there's no one around to sharpen it. Old varnish is removed first with varnish stripper and then the wood is scraped with a sharp scraper to bring back the natural color under the weathered surface. A file is used to sharpen the scraper as shown in the photograph (see below), cutting at an angle until a "rag" is raised on the opposite edge. This is then removed by laying the file flat against the back of the scraper blade and gently rubbing it away. Never sharpen a scraper with its point towards your hand. If the file slipped your hand would be carried on to the point.

There is only one golden rule for preparation. If the bare surface is smooth and glossy before you start painting, the final finish will be like porcelain. If it is scratched, scored and uneven the finish will be glossy, perhaps, but every scratch and unevenness will show plainly. You cannot cover blemishes with a multiple of coats.

After the scraping comes the sanding down, preferably done by an electrical power tool. The first rub down will be with fairly coarse garnet of carborundum paper, then the bare wood is primed, etc. Once the bare wood has been covered a wet-or-dry paper, used with water, is best. A cork block inside the paper

Once the preparation has been done the final touches can be applied. When boats are stored close together in a yard, it's not always easy to work the fitting-out program so that the boats near by are at the same stage

is used and all inequalities of surface must be ground away. After rinsing and when the surface is dry the "stopping" compound is larded on whenever needed and when this is dry sanded down again quite flat.

Remember to rub with the grain too, especially when old varnish is good enough to serve as the base for a couple of new coats. Rubbing down provides a roughened surface which will help the new varnish to "key" into the old and the same principle

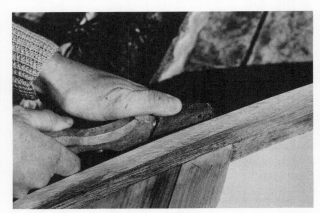

The golden rule is to scrape with the grain. This photograph shows clearly which way the grain is running. A good even pressure is essential, as is a sharp scraper, so master the art of sharpening the blade.

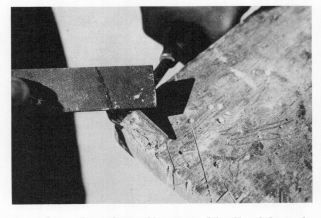

Sharpening a scraper. The point is away from the fingers so there is no risk of accident. Continue cutting at an angle until the underneath edge feels ragged, then remove the rag by laying the file against it and gently rubbing it away

applies to the repainting of an already well-painted hull, although in this case all scratches and hollows must be filled with stopper and rubbed down flat.

Paint and varnish brushes are expensive and not expendable. If they are left to harden they are ruined. Each time after use wash them in turpentine, then with detergent suds, rinse, and hang them in a tin of linseed oil. This will keep them in good condition indefinitely. Needless to say when a brush is to be used again the oil must be squeezed out and removed with turpentine, but this is a simple enough matter. Never dip more than half the brush in paint or varnish and apply it smoothly and evenly. The modern polyurethanes must be laid on quite thickly but be sure that you don't leave runs on vertical surfaces. Keep looking back to check this as the paint will harden quickly and brush marks will show up if left too late.

There are many tips to learn but here are some of the important ones. Don't get paint remover, or varnish remover, on plexiglass windows as it will eat into them. Don't let the point of your scraper score the plastic deck coverings when scraping along the edges of wooden deck fittings. (I've been guilty of both so I know how important these two are.) Don't paint or varnish on a windy day when dust is flying without first sprinkling water around the boat to settle the dust. In the early spring don't paint or varnish after 4:00 P.M. or dew may ruin the finish. Wrap some adhesive tape around the fingers which grip the brush—this will prevent painful blisters. Remove all dust completely after rubbing down and wipe over the surface with a turpentine-soaked rag. Don't paint or varnish damp wood. Keep a pair of rubber gloves especially for painting and a pair of stout gardening gloves for rubbing down. Boats are full of inaccessible corners which have to be painted and it is literally impossible to complete the fit-out without getting covered in paint, so keep old slacks, top, and shoes just for this purpose.

Fiber glass boats need painting after a few years, but unless the surfaces are roughened to remove wax and provide a keying surface, the paint will peel off again. Use coarse paper to remove old paint, then follow with a finer grade. Use special primer and polyurethane paint or epoxy paint on fiber glass.

Apart from helping with the outside preparation, the painting and the varnishing at fitting-out time, the sea wife will have charge of the down-below maintenance. If she is wise she will tackle her job systematically and by starting at laying-up time with a thorough clean-up below, emptying all lockers and leaving them open to air out through the winter, she can cut her spring work by half.

At lay-up time too the cooker can be cleaned and the parts greased, the water tank cleaned out, and the toilet serviced. All these jobs mean less work later on. Loose gear can be carted ashore—the cutlery, pots, pans, cushions, mattresses, sleeping bags, etc—leaving air circulating freely and the accommodation uncluttered so that any changes and improvements can be tackled freely.

Don't be too ambitious with improvements and, more important, don't add too many knickknacks—it's easy to become too fussy below. Simplicity and ease of working should be the aim; remember space below doesn't grow, but the bodies which fill it do.

10/Victualing the Galley

When sailing near shore, the cook depends on fresh provisions to a large extent, but for all that she might well have to call on the ship's stores from time to time. Perhaps there is no hope of getting ashore before the shops close; perhaps it is a holiday or the shops are just too inaccessible. Certainly on longer trips a great deal of food, fresh, dried, and canned, must be carried, not only for consumption on the trip, but because the cost of normal everyday stores can be quite prohibitive away from home.

Any smaller sailboat, whether she is used for day sailing, weekend or more extended cruising, or as a floating caravan in harbor, should be equipped with basic stores as well as a completely separate emergency stock. Here is a suggested list of basic stores to start the stock list rolling. Quantities, of course, depend on the number of crew, the amount of locker space available, and the length of sailing trips planned.

Tea	Bouillon	Canned meat
Coffee	Crackers	" fish
Sugar	Cookies	" milk
Dried milk	Instant cereals	" stews
Salt	Instant potatoes	" vegetables
Pepper	Packaged soups	" soups
Sauces	Rice	" puddings
Jelly	Dried vegetables	" fruit
Freeze-dried meals	Fruit drinks	" beverages

I have listed canned and dried soups and canned and dried milk because it is impossible to have too much of either. Canned soups are best when speed is essential, while the packaged variety,

129

which are easy to stow, are ideal when conditions are not quite so hectic.

These form the absolute basic, non-perishable stores; some items kept against real emergencies, others used regularly and replaced before they run out. Such things as instant coffee, crackers, a couple of cans each of, say, stew, soup, milk, beans, potatoes, rice, and fruit should be kept in a separate locker and left intact for real emergency. The wise cook will include matches and will stow these items in one of the less commonly used lockers —probably in a sealed box in the bilge and well away from the normal stores.

Incidentally, if possible choose imprinted cans, or otherwise devise some method of marking them before removing the labels. It may sound unnecessary, but it isn't. Labels left on cans, especially those cans stowed in the bilges, gradually disappear to clog up the bilge pump, but worse is to come. All unmarked cans look the same, so if you don't like canned spaghetti with rice pudding or peaches with Irish stew, heed this advice, mark the cans and keep the details of the different can markings quite safely.

Make a list of all the basic and emergency food stores and note any items used so that they can be replaced after each trip. In addition it is a good idea to add to the list such things as dish washing liquid, paper towels, cleaning powder, matches, toilet paper, etc. This means that when the time comes for restocking they won't be overlooked.

Once the stores are on board, the cook is free from worry. She knows there is food to feed a hungry crew if the occasion should arise. All she has to do now is keep the stock up and cater for each separate passage with her fresh stores as it comes.

Whether you are planning for a short passage or a long cruise it is a good idea to work out a rough menu. This doesn't necessarily have to be kept to religiously, but it will help with the victualing and is a basis on which to work. It is a good idea to take account of the weather outlook when planning the menu. Obviously if there has been a long, fine, warm spell and it looks like continuing, it is possible to include salads and be a bit more ambitious with the meals. On the other hand, in unsettled weather the best bet is to cater accordingly and include quickly prepared meals and such items as pie which can be eaten hot if you have an oven or cold.

When the menu has been worked out and the supplies bought, prepacking the items needed for each separate meal on passage in a plastic bag is a good arrangement. This means that everything for each meal—canned, fresh or dried—is easily available, and in the correct quantities, so that there is no need to forage in lockers, or in the bilge, which can be the final straw if the ship is at all lively.

Easy passage

In any case if she wants to get full enjoyment out of sailing and play her part in the running of the ship, the sea wife will have prepared most of her meals in advance for a short passage at sea. Aided by Thermos jugs she will have soup, stew or hot drinks to accompany each meal, sandwiches, crackers, cheese, cake, and fruit. In fact, something to suit each and every one of the crew from the most ravenous to the one who may be feeling the first qualms of seasickness.

If there is any likelihood of the passage being an extended one, she is still prepared with each meal packed so that it can be set out picnic fashion at the most suitable moment. This ensures the minimum of dish washing and fuss and the minimum of time in preparation. The second meal might include a hot dish again in a Thermos jug. Pre-cooked pie might follow and again crackers, and cheese and fruit for the not quite so hungry.

This type of meal and style of eating is very much in the tradition of the day sail and occasional night passage of the majority of small family sailors who sail weekend after weekend in this way during the season. More often than not the night is spent in a safe anchorage or on a mooring. Usually a good breakfast is prepared and eaten before the start of the return trip and once again the cook prepares her sandwiches and hot drinks before getting under way. On these trips the Saturday evening meal, when the craft is safely at anchor, is the highlight of the weekend and it is then that the cook can show off.

Before the start of the trip she knew pretty well what to expect; perhaps not from the weather, but she had a good idea of the length of the passage and, with her rough menu, catered accordingly. She brought all her weekend stores with her and apart from the general basics like sugar, tea, coffee, jelly, and condiments, didn't need to touch her canned or emergency stores at all, and right at the start she spent time stowing all the gear to make sure it all stayed in place at sea.

Hard passage

The same applies to the weekend passage which turns out to be a hard one. Again the cook prepares at least two meals in advance. In all probability if the weather is really rough, the crew will not be eating so much and more attention will be paid to grabbing the odd sandwich, crackers, the wedge of cake, cheese, etc. If hot drinks prove difficult, produce beer or fruit drink as thirst quenchers or, as cold sets in, the simplest of all hot drinks, bouillon. With luck the night will be spent in a safe harbor or

These are two Thermos bottles for liquids, but there are wide-mouthed jugs available for full meals

anchorage. If not, the real business of catering at sea begins.

Remember that early morning at sea, after a long, hard, cold night, catches people at their lowest ebb and this is the time for something simple to prepare, something hot and filling. I've found that hot cereal never fails, even among the squeamish, and with the latest instant Quaker Oats nothing could be easier. Follow with a hard-boiled egg and the crew have, at least, an adequate breakfast and enough to keep them going while the cook sorts herself out.

This photograph shows a set of non-stick pans—all stowed inside the biggest saucepan with frying pan on top. The lower photograph shows the full contents of the set

All this long night the ship has not been sailing herself. The owner at least, helped possibly by whoever is able to assist him at night, has been sitting out the long hours—and anyone who has sat out the graveyard watch alone will know how long the hours can be. This seems a good time to mention the cockpit "forage" box, the saving grace of many night watches; no cruiser that contemplates night passage should be without one. This should be kept handy in the cockpit and might include small packets of crackers or cookies, wrapped cheeses, wrapped cake, pies, chocolate, nuts, raisins, chewing gum, sweets. In fact as many small tempting items as it will hold and things, for the most part, which won't deteriorate with keeping. Most important, it must be kept stocked up.

The body is at its lowest ebb around 2:00 A.M. and it is then when hunger is felt by those who are awake throughout the night. Over and over again I have seen the change from a fit and hungry crew at 1:00 A.M. to a seasick, non-hungry crew at breakfast time. This was before we discovered the idea of the forage box and although I can't claim 100 percent success, it has worked in a good many cases. Naturally enough, hot drinks should also be available during the night, and for these vacuum flasks are obviously best since they can be left filled for when they are really needed.

Going back to the forage box. One other point in its favor: I've found that in the very worst weather, when cooking is out of the question, the breakfast can come out of it, but be warned, keep it for night sailing and for bad weather only and keep small prying fingers out of it.

Extended cruising

In normal sailing conditions cooking is a simple enough matter, but in rougher going quickly prepared meals, preferably meals cooked in one pan, are the answer. As a hot filler the stew/potatoes/beans type meal out of cans is hard to beat, certainly from the point of view of quickness. There are also a number of canned meals which are complete in themselves and well worth adding to the stores if this sort of sailing is to be undertaken very often. And, of course, packaged dried meals are a must in any galley.

In any case cooking in a seaway is never as difficult as it sounds. The old adage "you get used to anything in time" applies to sailing. Gradually the stomach settles down, the motion of the ship is taken in its stride and it is very, very rare for sickness to go on for over thirty-six hours. Nor, luckily, does bad weather usually last that long. By now, too, excitement will be mounting, the destination must be getting nearer and no greater fillip than this is needed to take minds off seasickness or hunger. The thought of shore meals, particularly if it is a foreign shore, will be enough to boost morale all round and make the discomforts of the passage fade.

That the whole business must be repeated on the way back is no dampener. The ship and the crew have done it once, the cook has coped with her task quite ably—the next time can never be so bad.

11/Feeding at Sea

All sailing wives know how to cook—or at least they know *what* they can cook. Taking into account different cooking arrangements available on small craft, here are some suggestions which should act as a guide to the type of meals which can be produced.

The first section deals with one-burner cookery and this is followed by cooking with two burners, two burners and grill, and more complicated dishes for sailboats with ovens. A section on dried food and Thermos jug cookery completes the chapter. I have not attempted to include recipes which rely on complicated equipment; to my mind there isn't room for fancy gadgets on the small sailboat. Nor have I included any recipes which require cooking in deep fat or in a lot of fat. My feeling is that any quantity of hot fat on a sailboat which goes to sea is an unnecessary and dangerous hazard and one we can manage without. In fact I have not included many recipes at all. I have made suggestions, leaving the rest to the sea cook's ingenuity.

One burner

The first necessity for a cook attempting to feed a hungry crew on one burner is a good-quality saucepan and steamer combined or double boiler. But be sure to see that it is secure against falling off the stove. With this and a bit of careful planning it is possible to cook a complete meal. Needless to say recipes will be fairly simple, but with a stew in the bottom, and canned vegetables and canned pudding in the top, the cook has a bulky enough meal for any hungry crew. In this case and whenever cans are put in the steamer the tops must be removed.

With this sort of cooking in mind a great deal of thought should be paid to getting the best steamer available; preferably one with separate sections, but an ordinary steamer with perforated base will do. This is when the use of foil to wrap the different foodstuffs (if they are fresh) pays off.

The saucepan can be used for braising, stewing, frying or boiling while the top takes canned foods of different sorts to accompany the main course or for the dessert. With practice and if she really enjoys cooking at sea the cook can take on much more complicated meals, even to sponge puddings in the top, but generally speaking this type of meal is more than adequate on a small sailboat.

A couple of recipes for one-burner cooking.

Sea Pie (bottom pan)
Canned Potatoes, Stuffed Apples (steamer)

Basis of Sea Pie is a normal beef stew, fresh or canned. Make a quantity of dough for the crust, divide into four and put on top of stew half an hour before cooking ends. Finish cooking with steamer on top. Apples are cored and stuffed with syrup, sugar or dried fruit and put into steamer with the potatoes when the crust goes on. They take 30 minutes to cook.

Curry (bottom pan)
Rice, Canned Fruit Pudding (steamer)

This time the rice is cooked before the curry, strained, then wrapped in foil ready for reheating in the steamer. The curry can be fresh or canned or dehydrated. The rice goes on top of the pudding in the steamer about half an hour before cooking time ends. This method with rice is quite foolproof.

From these recipes it can be seen that the variety of menus, using fresh, dried, canned or part precooked food, can be great. In addition the one-burner cook has her frying pan to take care of breakfasts, such things as omelettes, and to fry quick dishes such as hamburgers, steaks, and sausages to accompany the vegetables previously cooked with the pudding in the pan/steamer.

Two burners

With two burners the scope widens enormously, but with the extra flame a steaming pan is still a great asset. Now the cook can ring the changes. She can fry her meat, cook vegetables separately and make curry without having to precook the rice. A great many meals at home are produced on two hot plates so this is nothing new. The steamer can be used for heating the dessert or the meal livened up with fritters or pancakes fried on the second burner while the first course is in the pan/steamer. The two-burner cook can cope easily with breakfast and main meals, and, with the aid of a toast diffuser, flat grill or even an asbestos mat, can produce evening meals of the type of beans on toast, poached egg, scrambled egg on toast—in fact any toast-type snacks which don't need browning off.

This is something quite within the scope of the one-burner cook, too, although she will have to keep the toast hot, or the topping hot, while she tackles the other. Easier for her are the fried sandwich snacks which are always popular on board—Cheese Dreams, Fried Egg or Fried Bacon Sandwiches. These are good and filling, easily made, simple to eat and involve the minimum of preparation and dish washing.

CHEESE DREAMS

Butter two slices of bread on both sides. Sandwich together with a thick slice of cheese and fry in butter on both sides until golden brown. Treat egg or bacon the same way, cooking them first, of course.

Highly popular these with scouts and guides around the campfire, and they know a good body-filler when they see one.

For breakfast at sea the fried egg sandwiched between two pieces of bread is hard to beat. Remember to season the egg well and fry it on both sides. Needing no cooking at all are smoked fish. These cook themselves if immersed for five minutes in a pot of boiling water, but perhaps they should be kept for when the boat is safely at anchor.

Quick treats produced in the frying pan at various times, when people feel a bit peckish, all add up to keeping the crew happy, well fed, and not missing shore comforts too much. Surprise them with hot potato cakes (they can be made with dehydrated potatoes) or with pancakes. Both are usually cooked on a griddle, but a non-stick frying pan with a wipe of fat serves just as well.

I find that one of the most popular meals I produce on board is stuffed pancakes. Do these when the crew is fed in relays since pancakes are best eaten when they are just cooked. However, as the family settle down to the sailing routine, each doing their share of the deck duties and sailing the ship, meals are often taken in a more leisurely fashion with two people eating while the rest take over the sailing. It is at such times that this recipe finds favor. Stuff the pancakes with something out of a can like Chicken Supreme, or be daring, make a white sauce and add chicken, salmon, egg or shrimps. Many variations are possible, pancakes are good and filling, and they can be dressed up even more if accompanied by a thick tomato sauce.

To make a different type of stew, use canned or fresh chicken portions and a can of mushroom or chicken soup. Touched up a bit, particularly with a dash of sherry, it makes more of a party meal. Generally speaking specially made sweets, apart from quick things like pancakes and fritters, are too complicated to tackle on board. I reckon that if the cook puts all her talents to making the first course as interesting and as tasty as possible, something out of a can, fresh fruit, or crackers and cheese is more than ample for the dessert.

Two burners and grill

With the addition of a grill to the two-burner stove, there is probably no need for a steamer at all, but again it's up to the cook. Obviously she will be able to cope with more ambitious meals if she has a steamer too and, of course, if the steamer means that one burner can be used instead of two, gas is saved.

Now the sea cook can produce all the meals she wants. Perhaps the only items missing from her menus will be pies and baked dishes. She can grill meat, braise, stew, and boil, and she can finish off toasted snacks under her grill. In a pinch she can use the grill to warm up sausage rolls and small pies, provided she watches them carefully. In fact the only advantage the "oven" cook has over her is the question of baking and in keeping plates warm.

And it is a doubtful advantage. More often than not small ovens on small yachts—and space dictates that they must be small—are troublesome things and chancy to rely on. However, if the oven does work, the cook can arrive on board armed with ready-made pies, dishes such as meat pies, bread pudding, or any pie-type dish which tastes better hot. She can produce baked potatoes in their jackets at times when they warm the hands as well as the stomach and she can even buy frozen pies on her visits ashore and vary her menu greatly. There's no need to give her any recipes at all. She has all the conveniences of her shore kitchen afloat with her and anything she can do at home she can do on board.

Dried foods

So far I have made only brief mention of dried packaged meals which are now widely available for busy people ashore. Undoubtedly these fill a very useful function afloat, too. All the meals, including curries and stews (with rice or potatoes), risotto, chow mein, etc., take about 30 minutes to cook and they all need a bit of watching. However, a number of them do cook in one pan, which eases the one-burner cook's problems considerably.

I would say that these are the ideal meal for quieter days afloat or for the big event of the weekend, the Saturday evening meal at anchor. Certainly the curried meals which need a bit more care and attention, calling for rice to be strained, etc., would prove complicated in a seaway, but these are tasty meals with a great deal to recommend them. Ensure that there is a strainer on board, otherwise rice could be a problem.

Prepared meals are securely packed usually with each different item in its own aluminum envelope, clearly imprinted with cooking instructions. This means that to simplify stowage problems the outer carton can be scrapped so long as the different envelopes for each meal are kept together. These can then be stored on board all through the season with no fear of deterioration and they are a great safeguard against stocks running low. In all cases the correct volume of water added to the dried food is vital to the success of the meals, so a liquid measure of some sort is essential.

Still on the dried theme and doing away with the need for fresh potatoes on board altogether is the dehydrated potato now available from a number of firms. This makes up instantly into a vegetable to accompany the main meal or it can be used with tuna, corned beef, cheese, etc., as a good, quick and warming meal in its own right. Also on the market are dried peas and beans which take the minimum time to cook, and there is even a brand of "instant" dried peas which are ready to eat after two minutes' soaking in boiling water. Dried vegetables and onions are marketed which make a good tasty addition to stews and other meat dishes. You will nearly always find that the manufacturers of these dried foods print recipes on the package. Being quick and easy to prepare, these can be useful on board. Remember, though, that the instructions must be followed carefully, particularly as to soaking times. For example, instant potato may need soaking for only a minute, whereas sliced onions take 20 minutes in cold water and mixed vegetables 20 minutes in boiling water.

Anyway, here are some recipes which can be cooked on board or prepared ashore and finished off afloat; in each case cooking time is short.

Corned Beef Hash

1 package onion slices (soaked for 20 minutes, then drained)
1 can corned beef, cut in cubes
2 tablespoons butter or shortening
Good pinch mixed herbs
1 package instant potato flakes
Salt and pepper

Method: Drain onion slices and fry in fat until well colored. Add corned beef and herbs and fry together for one minute.

Meanwhile empty potato flakes into a bowl, add 1½ cups of cold water and stir gently to wet flakes. Leave for one minute to swell. Now add potato to the other ingredients and fry together, turning often, until golden brown.

TOMATO AND VEGETABLE RISOTTO

1 cup long-grain rice
2½ cups meat stock
½ package onion slices
½ package mixed vegetables
1 tablespoon tomato purée
4 tablespoons butter

Method: Soak onions in cold water for 20 minutes and mixed vegetables in boiling water for 20 minutes, drain both well. Fry onion in butter, without browning (a saucepan is best for this recipe), then add tomato purée and rice. Stir well until rice absorbs the butter—about 30 seconds. Tip in mixed vegetables and stock (boiling). Bring back to boil and stir once before putting on lid and allowing it to simmer for 15 minutes, by which time all the water will be absorbed. Don't stir at all while the rice is cooking, otherwise it will stick. This is a simple dish, but tasty and filling and of course it can be made more substantial by the addition of cold meat or poultry which should be put in at the same time as the stock.

CHILI CON CARNE

¾ lb. minced beef, previously cooked
1 package onion slices (soaked for 20 minutes in cold water, then drained)
1 teaspoon chili powder
1 small can baked beans in tomato sauce
1 teaspoon tomato purée
Pinch celery salt
½ cup beef stock
2 tablespoons butter

Method: Melt butter in frying pan. Add onions and cook gently, without browning for half a minute. Add tomato purée, chili powder, and minced beef. Stir well, then add stock and baked beans. Allow to simmer for 6 minutes, then season to taste and serve with instant potato.

Thermos jug recipes

Now to Thermos jug meals. All the way through I have mentioned hot meals in these, but of course, they will keep cold foods cold, too. In hot weather the diet can be varied a lot by filling the jug with ice cream, gelatin, iced tea, etc. The selection of vacuum jugs available from all the well-known makers is vast, but choose models with specially wide necks for main meals and preferably those divided into separate containers. Don't forget vacuum bottles for hot drinks and soups.

The following recipes have been brought out by one of the vacuum jug companies; they must be followed carefully, especially cooking times, because the food continues to simmer for up to an hour in the jug. Again these few recipes are just to start you thinking—any favorite stew or casserole dish can be part-cooked at home and transferred to a jug for finishing off and eating on board. Incidentally Thermos jugs keep food hot for up to eight hours and they work best if they are filled right up to the top. If, by any chance, the food doesn't fill the jug completely, top the available space up with boiling water for the best results.

CONTINENTAL MEAT BALLS AND NOODLES

Sauce
1 small onion peeled and finely chopped
2 tablespoons shortening
1 level teaspoon flour
1 level tablespoon tomato purée
1 cup water
½ level teaspoon salt
½ level teaspoon sugar

Meat Balls
¾ lb. lean minced beef
¼ level teaspoon thyme
Pepper
2 tablespoons fresh bread crumbs
2 tablespoons milk

Method, Sauce: Fry onion gently in fat until golden, stir in flour, and cook for 2 minutes. Remove from heat and blend in tomato purée and water. Season with salt and sugar, return to heat and slowly bring to boil, stirring. Reduce heat, cover pan and allow to simmer while preparing meat balls.

Meat Balls: Mix minced beef with thyme, salt, bread crumbs, and milk. Combine well and form into 24 small balls. Drop into sauce and simmer for 5 minutes only.

Rinse large, wide-mouth vacuum jug with hot water. Fill with meat balls and sauce then close lid securely. The meat balls will continue cooking for a further hour. Serve with buttered noodles which can be cooked for 7 minutes only before adding to another jug or cooked separately on board.

CHICKEN AND MUSHROOM CURRY

2 medium-sized onions, peeled and chopped finely
3 tablespoons shortening
1½–2 level tablespoons curry powder
1 level tablespoon tomato purée
½ cup mushrooms, peeled, washed, and chopped coarsely
1 cup warm water
½ level teaspoon powdered ginger
½ level teaspoon powdered cinnamon
½–1 level teaspoon salt
Bay leaf
3 level tablespoons sweet pickle
2 tablespoons seedless raisins
1 cup cooked chicken cut in chunks

Method: Fry onions in fat until golden, then stir in curry powder, tomato purée, and mushrooms. Gradually blend in water and remaining ingredients. Bring slowly to the boil, stirring continually, and cover pan. Simmer for 7 minutes *only.* Rinse large wide-mouth jug in hot water, fill with mixture and close securely. The curry will continue cooking for at least another hour. Serve with plain boiled rice. (Again this can be part cooked and put into a second jug for a complete instant meal.)

SWEET AND SOUR PORK

¼ lb. pork fillet, cut into cubes
1 level tablespoon flour
¼ cup onions

2 tablespoons shortening
½ cup cooking apple
2 level tablespoons sweet pickle
1 clove
1 level teaspoon salt
½ level teaspoon sage
1 teaspoon Worcestershire sauce
1 cup water
½ cup potato

Method: Toss cubes of pork in flour until well coated. Cut onions into paper-thin slices and lightly brown in fat. Add pork and fry briskly for a further 5 minutes. Mix in apple and potatoes—both coarsely crated—sweet pickle, clove, salt, sage, Worcestershire sauce. Gradually add water and bring contents to the boil, stirring. Reduce heat, cover pan and simmer gently for 20 minutes *only.* Then transfer to jug (30 oz. capacity) and close securely. This dish will be ready to eat in 3½ hours, but can be kept in the jug for up to 8 hours. Like all these Thermos dishes it serves four.

FLEMISH BEEF STEW AND RICE

¾ cup onions
1 clove garlic (optional)
2 tablespoons cooking fat
1 lb. stewing steak cut in 1-inch cubes
2 level tablespoons cornflour
1 cup beer
1 rounded teaspoon brown sugar
1 level teaspoon salt
black pepper

Method: Chop onion and garlic finely and brown in fat. Add meat and fry briskly for a further 5 minutes. Meanwhile mix cornflour to a thin paste with beer, add sugar and salt and pour into pan with the meat. Cook slowly, stirring, until contents come to the boil and thicken. Reduce heat, cover pan and allow to simmer for 15 minutes *only.* Season with salt and pepper and transfer immediately to Thermos jug and fasten securely. The stew will be ready to eat in 3½ hours and can be left in the jug for up to 8 hours. If the rice is to be

kept in a jug it should be boiled in salted water for 15 minutes
before draining and transferring to a separate jug.

A few useful dodges

When water is scarce, it may be necessary to use seawater for
cooking or dish washing, but only well offshore and away from
harbors. Any root vegetable can be boiled in seawater, but
remember no extra salt will be needed as flavoring. Personally,
if there is any doubt about water lasting out, I prefer to use
seawater for washing dishes only and stick to fresh water for
vegetables. However, when it is necessary to cook potatoes in
seawater they are best boiled in their skins. Never wash lettuce
in seawater, it goes limp. In any case, lettuce, chicory, celery,
tomatoes, and fresh fruit should be washed before they come on
board and then kept in plastic containers. Best stowage for small
tomatoes is an eggbox, by the way. It keeps them from bruising.

In a pinch, rice and pasta can be cooked in seawater, but only
in dire emergency, since it gets rather gooey. Never boil seawater
in the kettle and always rinse cups and mugs in fresh water after
they have been washed in salt, otherwise the next drink will be
ruined. Whether washed in salt or fresh water plastic mugs get
stained. There is a special cleaner on the market, but toothpaste
works just as well. Never use an abrasive, though; it ruins the
surface.

Did you know that a lump of butter in the water stops
vegetables from boiling over; that toast can be made on an
asbestos mat on the top of the stove; that bread and cakes keep
for ages wrapped in aluminum foil and that, in any case,
stone-ground bread lasts almost indefinitely? The uses of
aluminum foil are endless. When steaming several different items
together it can be used to wrap them separately to keep the
flavors from getting mixed. Remember to extend the cooking time
a bit. In fact pies and a good many other things can be wrapped
in foil and warmed through on an asbestos mat on top of the
stove (they will need careful watching), and food can even be
boiled in foil so long as it is wrapped very securely.

12/Children Afloat

The sailing mother who takes her children afloat must be capable of taking full charge of them above deck and below. The owner/husband will be fully occupied with the sailing and seamanship side, particularly when under way. Mother must see that the children are properly dressed for the various passages and that orders are followed implicitly. In fact, it will be up to her to ensure that the owner is free from worry and able to give all his concentration to sailing so that there are none of those sudden panics and alarms which all too easily dismay and frighten children who do not appreciate what they are all about.

Apart from the question of inflexible feeding times, toilet arrangements, etc., tiny children who can be safely tucked into baskets present no real problems. At the other end of the scale, children of from, say, eight upwards, used to boats and the sea, can become useful members of the crew, providing their interest can be kept alive. It is the in-betweens, the crawlers, the toddlers, the questers, who present the greatest problems. This is the age when children begin to copy, when they show eagerness to help with all the jobs on board; let them, and select some of the more simple tasks which they can handle by themselves.

So long as sailing is not thrust down their throats, to the exclusion of everything else, children brought up on the family sailboat, in a happy family atmosphere, take it all in their stride. This is the time when some careful thought about the type of sailing most likely to attract really young children is needed. Children are easily frightened and in any case they quickly become bored, so the wise skipper will not undertake any prolonged passages until they are used to the sea, confident in the ability of the parents and boat to cope with whatever might arise and settled into a sailing routine.

All this takes time, of course, and parents who are looking ahead to years of happy family participation in the sport should be patient and spend the first weeks, months, maybe even season, on short picnic cruises, with plenty of trips ashore, swimming, fishing, and exploring. The occasional night away or longer passage might be fitted in if the weather is good and settled. With proper groundwork, patience will be rewarded and without much lost time a happy, well-trained family crew will be embarking on longer trips, well fitted to cope with longer sea passages and looking forward keenly to the adventure of *real* family sailing.

From the very beginning a child has to learn what is right aboard a boat and what is wrong. The lesson of complete and immediate obedience must also be put across, but from the very start explain the whys and wherefores of the rules. Give a practical demonstration of why the mainsheet must be kept clear; why the head must be kept down when jibing and going about; why there is only one way to step aboard a dinghy. A practical demonstration of all these points and any others that spring to mind, although painful, is the surest guarantee of obedience I know. Go a stage further and turn the dinghy over (choose a nice warm day and shallow water) and try out man-overboard drill, too. There's no better way of getting the message across, but don't make a tense, frightening fuss about it. Above all, make sailing enjoyable for all the family and if at some stage the keenness of one or more of the crew seems to be waning, leave them ashore with relatives while the rest of the family go. So long as they are not forced to join in they will soon feel they are missing out on the family trips and show eagerness to join in again.

Just as the saying goes that a man needs an extra foot of boat for every year of age, so it is said that the duration of a sail should be in strict relationship to age, certainly as far as children are concerned. That is to say a ten-hour passage for a ten-year-old and so on. Down the scale a five-hour passage for a five-year-old, unless part of the time is spent asleep, is more than enough; and it is very rare for a child of this age to remain interested for such a period.

Proof that lifejackets for tiny babies really are available. This youngster, less than six months old, finds the motion of the boat soothing and sleeps through anything

Children's safety

The safety of their children is probably the greatest worry to sailing parents; and although the dangers afloat always seem much worse than shore-side dangers, in actual fact so long as the rules are observed, children are considerably safer at sea than they are playing at home, or crossing streets. The first rule, of course, is obedience, immediate obedience to all commands, and this must be instinctive. There's no doubt a disobedient child afloat is in continual danger and unless willing obedience can be taught everyone on board will be in a constant state of tension.

The wearing of lifejackets must be automatic. Before a child steps into a boat of any sort, dinghy tender, launch, cruiser, what-have-you, the jacket must go on. Here parents can do a great deal to help. As mentioned earlier, children love to copy, so the whole business of lifejackets should be something shared by all the family, part of the "dressing-up" prior to going afloat, in fact. This is just as important for older children whether they can swim or not, although later on as the swimming child becomes more used to sailing the rule can be relaxed somewhat in quieter weather and at anchor or on moorings. Of course the temperature of the water will have a great bearing on whether or not a swimming child should be made to wear a lifejacket.

Mother is a keen sailor and the baby certainly doesn't stop her going to sea or joining in the sailing. Just visible is a portable seat (rather like a baby's car seat), and once the baby is secured in this —either in the cockpit or below—the parents are free to relax and enjoy the sailing

The cockpit and the cabin are obviously the places for children when sailing, and when in the cockpit small children should always wear a safety harness—again even at anchor or on moorings. Sooner or later the adventurous child will go overboard, but so long as a lifejacket and/or safety harness is worn and there is a dinghy handy, there should be no difficulty at all in getting him back again quickly and easily. Equally important, whenever a child is in the cockpit or on deck, a grown-up should always be around to keep an eye open.

Really tiny babies are rarely seasick, in fact they enjoy the motion of the ship; but older children are just as susceptible to seasickness as grown-ups. This is another reason why longer

This child's safety harness has a special double safety device which makes it proof against prying fingers

This youth's safety harness is suitable for weights up to 140 pounds. Manufacturers have produced numerous safety items for children

passages should only be undertaken when children have become used to sailing and coping with seasickness when it happens. Treat seasickness as perfectly normal, but don't discuss it too much in front of children. Sleep is the best cure for seasick children, so give one of the sleep-inducing tablets and tuck them in below. Ten to one they'll wake up refreshed, hungry and quite fit again.

Clothes for children afloat

Keeping children warm and dry is vitally important. Several firms specialize in tough sailing clothing for children and miniatures of most of the grown-up models are available. Like grown-ups children should have plenty of warm woollen clothes to wear under wind and waterproof suits. Waterproof suits should be big enough to take all the extra clothes worn underneath and to allow for growing. They should be chosen for ease of putting on and taking off, and the jacket should have a hood to protect the head and neck against wind and water. Another good hat which comes well down over the ears is a good bet for cold, rainless days; and the child should have a towel scarf for the neck, good woollen gloves, socks and—an absolute must, this—proper non-slip shoes. Although non-slip shoes in children's sizes are not easily available a number of firms specialize in them and every effort should be made to get them. The only safe alternative to non-slip shoes is bare feet—which is all very well in hot weather but not so good in cold. Also, there is the danger of stubbed toes.

A sun hat which protects the head and the eyes from glare is a must for summer sailing and at this time too a lightweight parka or canvas jacket for keeping out cool breezes is an asset. Needless to say one complete change of clothes is essential at all times.

Lifejackets, buoyancy aids, harnesses

Choice of lifejacket needs very careful consideration. Remember the child will have to wear the aid for hours on end so freedom

Three tough, lightweight suits. Remember to choose suits big enough to allow for growing and for extra layers of clothes, as well as for freedom of movement

of movement and comfort must be the first considerations. The alternative, usually either kapok-filled or inflatable (and the latter would have to be worn fully inflated since a child would not be able to inflate it in the water), are extremely bulky and would not be a practical proposition in a relatively small sailboat. To my mind it's more important for a small child to wear a safety harness at all times when on deck or in the cockpit. This should certainly be a hard and fast rule until he or she is able to swim at least 50 yards and is at home in the water and will not panic when out of his depth.

(There are imported jackets that are not bulky or restricting to body movement and yet provide satisfactory buoyancy. However, many foreign-made jackets are not approved by the U.S. Coast Guard. Motorboats, auxiliary sailboats, and even sailboats under most state laws are required to carry at least one life-saving device for each person aboard.)

When it comes to buying buoyancy equipment, consult the experts and try on different models. Manufacturers have devoted

Good tough sailing suit and kapok buoyancy aid. Whatever type of life-jacket is worn, ensure that it is correctly fastened at all times

a great deal of thought and attention to incorporating the various standards into buoyancy aids for children (there are even buoyancy vests available for tiny babies) and will know the best type available for your particular needs.

This applies to safety harnesses, too, and these are also available in children's sizes. Once again make certain the child is happy and comfortable in the model chosen, but this time pay just as much thought and attention to ease in putting on and taking off. Some harnesses are very complex and difficult to sort out quickly when time is short. Don't forget there should be good strong attachments in the cockpit for harnesses and perhaps one or two down below as well. To begin with put small children on short lines until they find their sea legs and lengthen the scope as they become more used to life afloat and what they can and cannot do. The importance of safety harnesses cannot be too heavily stressed—they are vital if sailing parents are going to have any peace of mind at all.

Coping with children in their various age groups

Babies. Luckily the basket acts as a carriage, cot, playpen—the lot—and solves a good many problems when taking babies afloat. The main problem is finding safe stowage for the basket below and in the cockpit when sailing. It should be wedged in securely on a bunk below to stop it from slipping and sliding around, and you should choose a place where there is some fresh air, but no danger of the occasional dollop of spray. Secure fastening in the cockpit is not quite so easy, but by means of chocks and a rope lashing it is possible to fix the basket so that it stays put. Preferably it should be fixed amidships in the cockpit, with the baby lying fore and aft, otherwise the basket will have to be moved over each time the ship is tacked.

Disposable diapers, ready-prepared canned baby foods and milks make feeding and looking after the tiny baby a simple matter. Probably the biggest item of equipment will be the bath, but an ordinary plastic bowl serves the purpose well enough. To

This eight-year-old started in at the deep end. From her first sail she joined in the work on board—rowing the dinghy, helping with sails and, on quiet days, beginning to get the feel of the tiller. The sailing suit was chosen with future years in mind and since this wearer argued about a life vest her parents compromised by letting her wear it beneath the jacket

my mind disposable sheets and pillow cases, such as are made in Finland from specially treated rayon, are the ideal answer for babies and tiny children afloat. The sheets are full-size, but they can be cut to fit; they are tough and take up very little space indeed.

Unlike older children, babies do not need amusing, but they do need careful watching. Remember the sun's glare from the water is particularly strong, so don't expose the tiny baby to too much sun afloat, and remember that sea breezes are drying and burning and they can also be very chilling.

Crawlers and toddlers. There's no problem about sleeping accommodation for the slightly bigger child. They take to bunks very rapidly, and, in fact, two small children can be tucked into one bunk (not a quarter berth, of course) with no trouble at all. Naturally, tiny children will need a bunk canvas or board to keep them securely tucked in. In any case, whether there's a bunk canvas or not, it is a good idea to wedge them in thoroughly with cushions so that they don't roll around as the ship moves. There are specially small sleeping bags available, but since children grow quickly this is not altogether a practical idea. A better arrangement is to make up a blanket bag for them and buy a full-size sleeping bag as soon as they are big enough.

Small children, unless they are of the particularly nervous type, sleep through almost anything afloat, so if any longer passages are envisaged it is often a good idea to make them at night when the small ones are asleep below. The snag about this is that when the sailors are feeling tired after an all-night vigil, healthily refreshed children are wide awake, agog for the start of a new day.

At this age amusement is needed, and a good supply of toys. Choose floating dolls and animals for preference and books which are expendable, or at least cloth books which are proof against water. Include one or two teaching toys which can be played with on the cabin or cockpit floors. Children in this group must wear lifejackets at all times when out of their bunks and safety harnesses in the cockpit and on deck.

Toilet arrangements at this stage are simple. No child minds

What is in store for this family? They've had their sail and are now keen to enjoy the delights ashore. The skipper seems undecided whether to go alongside or nose up to the shore. Whatever the choice, the children are sensibly clad and prepared for anything

missing out on a bath for a few days, and using a plastic pot should present no difficulties.

Fours to eights. The age of curiosity and copying. Providing children wear lifejackets at all times and harnesses when venturing into the cockpit and on deck they should be allowed to help with the simple tasks and given time at the helm, if they show the inclination. Start teaching them simple knots, begin swimming lessons, and if they are learning to swim ashore give them as much practice as possible during the weekends. Learning to swim in a pool is one thing, but children should start getting used to swimming in wavelets and in tidal conditions as soon as possible.

If they show interest take time to explain what is happening, why a thing is done a certain way. Let them see you sticking to the rules they are expected to keep. Naturally there will be times of boredom and amusements will be needed. Get some educational books on the sea, buoys, flags, seabirds, boats of various classes, etc., so that they can do their own spotting. Puzzles, card games, and books are a must. A cheap fishing line is also an asset when it comes to keeping children occupied while sailing. A towing toy of some sort also helps at this time.

Fit in plenty of trips ashore, picnicking, fishing, bathing, and on these trips begin rowing lessons if children are interested. But right from the start teach proper dinghy routine, getting on board, behavior on board, and leaving the dinghy.

Sleeping arrangements are just the same as for smaller children, with older children occupying a whole bunk if space permits. Teach them the proper routine with the marine toilet, show them how it works, explain why knobs are turned, and so on. Taking in the information gradually like this, as equipment is used, they soon acquire a good all-round knowledge of the routine afloat.

Over eights. Children of eight and upwards who are used to boats can be really useful on board; those introduced to sailing more recently can be just as useful provided they are allowed to join in and help right from the start. Trust them to help with the various jobs, as this way they learn in double-quick time. Once again the lifejacket is a must in the cockpit, as is the safety harness on deck, especially when sailing. This is the age of the why and the wherefore, but however much curiosity a child shows the golden rule holds good—instant obedience to orders.

Again arrange lots of shore-side trips, bathing, exploring, etc., and have plenty of books on board. Teach knots, splices, whippings, and the principles of sailing, and above all let the child of this age discover the dinghy and, having learned how to row, let him venture off alone on trips ashore. Naturally a child, however capable in a dinghy, must wear a lifejacket, and if the dinghy is not already fitted with its own built-in buoyancy, as it should be, it should be equipped with buoyancy bags big enough to keep it afloat if it should turn over.

Once a child has gained confidence in a dinghy, a great stride has been made. In fact a lot of children consider the dinghy duties their own special jobs, taking over the trips ashore, the journeys back and forth with gear and provisions, thus relieving the older members of the crew of at least one chore. What is important is that by learning how to handle the dinghy properly the child has assimilated a tremendous amount of basic seamanship,—for example allowing for wind and tide when tying up alongside or

A quiet morning and a shallow shore—ideal conditions in which to start handling the dinghy. This girl was rowing, on the sea, when she was six and was soon able to maneuver alongside and take over the trips to the shore

There are many jobs older children can tackle. This one made heavy weather of hoisting the burgee, but it arrived at the masthead in due course and this was just one more job mastered. Gradually the knowledge builds up and soon children become really useful members of the crew

making for the shore, as well as certain right of way rules. In fact he has had his first lesson in seamanship, which once learned will never be forgotten.

Remember, though, that even at this age boredom soon sets in, so never expect too much in the way of long-term interest. Always have some alternatives up your sleeve, and keep the food as interesting as possible; appetites will be hearty and, at times of boredom, meals will be the highlight of the day. Above all let children help down below and in the galley if the deckside chores have lost interest. Who knows, you may not have a top-notch deckhand in your crew, but you may have a first-rate sea cook.

Do's and don'ts for children afloat

Never let children copy father and try to draw water from over the side. The sudden tug as the bucket fills, whether large or small, could easily pull them overboard. This is just as important at anchor or at moorings. The tide on some coasts is sometimes sufficient in itself to give a hard enough pull to catch a child unawares.

Never allow children to swim from a boat unless there is someone on deck to watch them, a dinghy in the water and a ladder rigged to help them on board again. Anyone who has tried to get even a very light person on board from the water will confirm how difficult this can be. In any case, a child should never be encouraged to swim from the boat, except at fairly slack tide. The tide is usually stronger than you think.

Never allow children to climb around on deck unless there is someone watching them all the time. When they do, make them abide by the standard rule for all yachtsmen—a hand for yourself and one for the ship. Once this becomes instinctive children are halfway to becoming seamen. It is a rule that applies to grown-ups, too.

Keep to the rules about wearing lifejackets and safety harnesses scrupulously so that they become automatic.

Make it a rule for children to wear waterproofs every time they go on deck at sea, unless it is very calm. A dry, warm child can enjoy the thrill of sailing; a wet, cold one soon begins to feel the effects not only of prolonged cold but of seasickness, too.

Keep calm at all times. Panic is contagious and frightening to the already nervous child.

Boost the skipper/owner, show that you have confidence in him and his decisions, thus instilling the same confidence in the children.

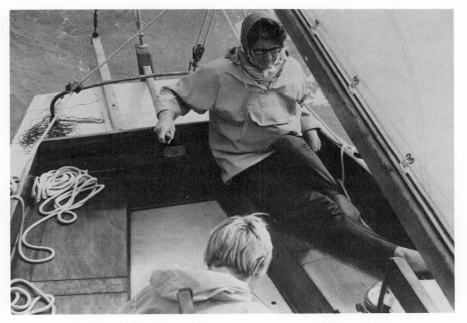

A gentle breeze, quiet sailing and a typical cockpit scene. The attraction of the fishing line has palled. This eight-year-old soon took to sailing, but for all that a passage of six or seven hours was about as much as she could cope with at one time

Keep a selection of games, books, puzzles as an emergency stock for really bad days. Bring them out as a surprise when all else seems to have failed.

Keep a watchful eye open for the first stages of seasickness. Try an anti-sickness tablet, a few drops of lemon juice or glucose, and cut out fatty foods as much as possible.

It's not good enough just to wear lifejackets, they must be properly secured at all times. Make the habit completely automatic and teach children the right way to lace them up and tie them right from the beginning.

A knot which is wrongly tied is dangerous afloat. Any knot a child makes, on his lifejacket or securing the dinghy, must be right. Start by teaching two simple knots like the reef and the round turn, two half-hitches, and then enlarge upon them.

When afloat watch for eyestrain in the glare and for sunburn or windburn. These can make an otherwise enjoyable cruise misery.

Show older children what the life buoy is for. Demonstrate how it should be thrown and explain why. One day they may see someone in trouble and quick action may be needed.

13/Beauty Care and Clothes

Aids to beauty afloat

Most women look their best tanned and with the healthy glow which an active life gives them; just as many find the slightly windblown look becoming. However, there is a happy mean in all things. What starts as a healthy windblown look all too soon develops into tough, weatherbeaten skin, permanent wrinkles round eyes, and dry hair—to say nothing of calluses on hands and ruined nails.

No woman is welcomed afloat if her prime concern is her appearance, since this usually entails a massive array of lotions and beauty aids. By the same token the majority of men like their handy sea-mates to look almost band-box fresh even when they step ashore after an arduous sail. Luckily we don't all expect to look like movie stars, so the overall effect can be achieved with a little care and a good deal of forethought.

I would put hair care as first priority because no matter how long a woman spends on her face, if her hair is a mess she can do very little about it afloat—and she knows it. At all times wear a good wide hair band at least, or a head scarf or hat (preferably one which doesn't flatten the hair too much). This is a way of ensuring that the hair keeps in order and it also goes a long way to protecting it against the very drying air. A good stringent lotion that can be rubbed into the hair at night helps a great deal. Short hair or hair long enough to tie back or pin up is obviously best at sea, above and below deck, and the woman who owns a hair-piece and is practiced at fixing it herself is way ahead when it comes to ringing the changes for that important visit ashore. However, I would never advocate taking a wig—there isn't room on board the small sailboat for items like this.

Skin need not become weatherbeaten, particularly when most family sailboats are only away for weekends or an occasional longer time. The basic essential is a good moisturizing cream under makeup at all times and a good cold cream at night. Most women find this is as much as they can cope with anyway, especially when they have children on board. Guard lips against chafe and apply a lip salve at night and before applying lipstick. Watch the eyes and if the sun or glare from the sea is strong wear sunglasses or a hat with a shading brim. I would put Murine, or something like it, high on the list for refreshing tired eyes, although cold tea, if it's handy, does the job very well and is good for a hot, tired face, too.

Hands suffer more than anything else at sea, mainly because we deal with very small quantities of water and they are never deeply immersed as they are at home. A good barrier cream applied at regular intervals during the day, rubber gloves for the rougher jobs below, and sailing gloves for on deck go a long way to keeping hands reasonably smooth. In addition to barrier cream have one of the dirt solvent cleansers handy. Some jobs defy all other cleaners and ten to one the skipper's hands will be in need of attention before he is fit to go ashore. Invest in one of the best hand creams available for night time and whenever you use a lemon keep the bits for rubbing over hands, elbows, and knees; it's a great softener. By the way, although ideally gloves will be worn for most of the jobs on deck, there's still no place for long nails on boats. Keep them to a sensible length and for preference choose a natural or pale varnish, which if it gets chipped never looks as bad as vivid colors.

Milk is a good emergency face cleanser and astringent, but always keep a face pack handy on board; it could be just the pick-you-up needed when a invitation to a special party ashore comes out of the blue. Incidentally, white of egg with a few drops of milk makes a good face pack. To save on water buy a large box of cleansing pads; when things are getting hectic and time is short a quick face-clean and makeup gives a tremendous boost to morale.

Equally important, watch the tan. A nice light brown glow all too quickly turns into a deep leathery skin which cracks and peels. Apply suntan cream regularly whether there is sun or not. It protects against harsh winds just as well as the sun's glare.

Shore-going clothes

For nine-tenths of the time shore-going clothes will be tucked away in lockers so they must be chosen for their crease-resistant properties as well as their ease in stowing. Luckily modern man-made fibers have eased the problem enormously and the choice of light, absolutely uncrushable materials is wide. Shore-going clothes should look right for all occasions, but choose sensible colors which won't show every speck of dirt. A top garment—jacket, cardigan or lightweight full length coat—to protect you on late cool evenings is essential, and personally I think a waterproof wrap-around skirt (like those worn by women golfers) is vital protection on trips to and from shore in the dinghy. Otherwise, how do you sit down?

Shore-going shoes need some thought. Rubber soles are a must because they will be worn on board, in the dinghy, on jetties and on beaches ashore. Flats or small comfortable heels are best and the uppers should be salt-proof. Needless to say, high-heeled shoes are out and so for that matter are tight skirts which restrict movement. Taking advantage of modern fashion, culottes provide the best and most respectable answer. Let's hope they are here to stay.

Quite a lot of sailing women stick to slacks for going ashore. Perhaps they are wise, for more often than not trips ashore are undertaken in cold, rough, wet conditions. There's no doubt about it, good tailored slacks, again in a crease-proof material, look good and workman-like, but choose a color which doesn't show every speck of dirt and keep them for going ashore only. Worn on board they soon acquire the well-worn, faded, baggy-knee look which is all too familiar. Remember, though, some restaurants and clubs insist on skirts in the evenings and ties for the menfolk, so it's probably safer to stick to these when venturing into new areas.

Handbags, the normal ones used ashore, are completely wrong

Nothing looks smarter or more nautical than navy and white, and when it
is teamed with a reefer jacket with
brass buttons it is right for any occasion ashore. Remember shore-going
clothes spend much of their time
tucked in lockers, so they should be
chosen with this in mind

His and her outfits with a nautical
touch. This is an example of how
good well-cut trousers and striped
tops can look. The slip-over top is
just right for cooler dry days afloat
or for teaming with skirts for cool
evenings ashore

afloat. Stick to a canvas bag or a good stout plastic one and make
sure it is big enough to take all the extras a visit ashore entails
—flashlight, oarlocks, protective clothing, perhaps even spare
shoes, to mention but a few. Beach bags are also essential for
family visits ashore, but again make sure they are plenty big
enough and will expand to take all the swimming gear and the
picnic things, towels, extra warm clothing and all the rest. Just
as important, they should fold up small so that they can be tucked
into the smallest locker when not in use.

Clothes for seagoing

When it comes to deciding on the top layer of clothing for seagoing a lot of points have to be taken into account. Any sailing suit, whether it is one piece or two, thick or thin, must be completely wind and waterproof. The sailing suit is not expected to give warmth, it is for protection only. Warmth comes from layers worn underneath and it is the number of layers, not the thickness of individual garments, which gives warmth, say the experts.

Once again modern synthetic materials have enabled manufacturers to produce hard-weather sailing gear which will stand up to the most rigorous conditions afloat. For small craft sailing, nylon or Dacron based materials probably serve best since being lighter they take up less space and they are virtually tear-proof. Make sure that all seams are welded, or treated—stitching alone is not waterproof. Wrists and trouser bottoms should have storm cuffs and the front opening, whether fitted with zip, stud, or buttons, should also have a double or storm fastening of some sort. A great deal of time will be spent sitting in water or at least on wet seats, so the bottom should have a reinforced panel and again the seams should be welded. Neck fastening is just as important and although hoods are not all that comfortable for looking around and feeling the direction of the wind, they are the only real answer to keeping water from getting down the back of the neck in the worst conditions.

Many people like one-piece suits, jackets, and trousers, but I think the two-piece suit is best for small boat sailing. The top can be worn separately in conditions which make the trousers unnecessary and the two piece is much easier to get on and off in the confined space of the cabin. I prefer the jacket top that has no fastenings down the front, which means there is less likelihood of water getting in at the front.

When buying a sailing suit, remember the layers of clothing which will be worn underneath and make certain it is plenty big enough. Just as important, see that the trousers come well up and the top well down otherwise water could get between the two.

Ideally the trousers should be elasticized at the waist so that they stretch over the extra layers yet still remain snug and the jacket

One of the most popular outfits among women sailors—the sailing suit with a jacket top. This one in red nylon has an attached hood, drawstring waist and a good deep pouch pocket

should have a drawstring at the bottom as well as at the neck. Good big pockets in the top are vital to take all the oddments one collects, so steer clear of any sailing outfits without them.

Choose a color which will show up—light colors stand out at night; yellow, orange and red show up best in the water. In any case make sure it is a color you will be happy in. A seasick person in green or blue looks ghastly.

Personal buoyancy

Some sailing jackets incorporate their own built-in buoyancy in one form or other, some with trapped-in air or foam-filled pockets, others which are fully inflatable. These ease the problem of personal buoyancy a great deal since a jacket with its own built-in buoyancy is in effect two garments in one. Each time the jacket is put on the buoyancy is put on, and there is no problem about deciding when conditions warrant a buoyancy aid. However, in most cases such jackets are swimming aids only. The exception is when the inflatable jacket is worn fully inflated. In this case the buoyancy is there but the jacket is probably too bulky for active and comfortable wear on a small sailboat. Obviously a compromise has to be reached.

The ideal on small sailboats, whether they venture far offshore or not, is to have a buoyancy aid for each member of the crew (either built into a sailing jacket or as a separate garment) and a Coast Guard approved lifejacket for real emergency.

The question of choosing a comfortable model is just as important for grown-ups as it is for children. An active, busy life on deck and just as active and busy a life in the confined space below make lack of bulk of paramount importance, so a lot of time should be spent in searching for the different types available, trying them on for comfort and deciding which offer the best protection for the sort of sailing planned while still considering ease of stowing below.

Safety harnesses

Ideally there should be a safety harness on board for each member

One-piece suit for the man, plus
short non-slip boots. The boy wears
a suit with a jacket top, the girl has
a button-through jacket. They all
have hoods attached

Doubly safe. These two are wearing
personal buoyancy vests and safety
harnesses. These vests show that
buoyancy aids can be designed to
give buoyancy without bulk

of the crew. These should be used at the skipper's discretion. All
the crew should know where they are stowed (this goes for
emergency lifejackets too) and how they work, and non-swimmers
should be encouraged to wear them as a matter of course when
working on deck in choppy conditions. Everyone on board should
know where the strong points for attaching the lines are to be
found and should practice wearing a harness and moving around
on deck from one attachment to another in quiet weather in
readiness for the real test.

Clothes for warmth

Underneath layers should never be tight—clothes which allow a passage of air around the body give better warmth, and keeping warm afloat is the aim. Coldness brings in its train seasickness, depression, and tiredness and no one suffering in this way can really pull their weight. Clothes for wearing afloat must be chosen wisely. There is a limit to the number of items which can be carried so each garment must do the job for which it was intended and do it well.

To cope with really cold days and long nights at sea a thermal undersuit in 100 percent nylon pile is ideal. Rather like a track suit, it gives an insulating layer of warm air if worn with the soft pile next to the skin. It can also be worn on top of other clothing as an additional layer for a good degree of warmth. There are also two-piece suits that look rather like pajamas, which are excellent.

Two examples of thermal suits. They can be worn on top of other under-clothes, but since they build up a layer of warm air next to the skin, they are really all that is needed under sailing suits

Tights, good hard wearing slacks or jeans, and long sweaters which come well down over the hips (thick or thin depending on the time of the year) make up the basic below-sailing-suit wear, but it is probably a good idea to include a lightweight canvas jacket or parka to keep out the wind on the less arduous days afloat.

Smaller items such as T-shirts, blouses, a neck towel to protect against water getting in, and a woollen sailing hat—preferably one which pulls well down over the ears, to protect the head in conditions when the sailing hood is not needed—make up the rest of the sailing gear. This last item is essential; remember the head loses more heat than any other part of the body. Summer sailing might well see the addition of a sun hat, shorts, tops and swimming gear. However, when such gear is carried some of the heavier clothing items can be left ashore, since space is always at a premium.

Special sailing gloves with stippled rubber pads on the fingers and thumbs make it possible to handle sails and ropes when wearing gloves, but as far as warmth goes woollen gloves serve best since they remain warm even when wet. Perhaps better still are the neoprene wet-suit gloves now available. These work on the same principle as wet-suits and providing the hands start warm, keep them warm even when wet.

Non-slip deck shoes are essential and, if space permits, I would put non-slip boots high on the list too. Not only do they protect the feet on board, but also they are useful for visits ashore, launching and beaching dinghies, etc. Choose boots and shoes big enough to take thick socks and also carry at least one spare pair of socks in your kit.

Talking of spare gear. A good basis on which to work is one spare set of everything—trousers, sweater, shorts, shirt, as well as underwear. Good warm pajamas, preferably a dark color, are best. You never know when a sudden emergency might mean a dash on deck, so they should pass muster and be warm, too.

To carry all the gear a handy zipped hold-all or a duffle bag (in stout plastic or canvas) and a smaller one for personal gear should see you fit for anything the weatherman might dish up.

14/First Aid and Sanitation

Unless the sailing wife knows a limited amount about handling the ship her husband is in a very vulnerable position indeed. Just imagine what might happen if he were hit over the head and knocked unconscious, even for a few minutes. It was the thought of this sort of emergency which, more than anything else, prompted me to tackle this book.

Serious accidents aboard boats are rare, but the consequences of even minor mishaps can be grave. A knock on the head which renders the skipper unconscious for a few minutes may not be serious to him; but it could well be serious to the ship and the crew if there is no one on board to take charge. However, the cure for this is not to be found in this chapter—it lies in basic seamanship, ship handling, and navigation, all dealt with earlier.

Certainly the wife who sails regularly with her husband should ask herself, honestly, if she could cope were she left in sole charge —say heave-to, or keep the boat quietly jogging along while she tended the wounded? Keep her sailing on course, free from danger, for a few minutes or until help was at hand? Get safely back to port if need be? Run the ship under guidance, and smoothly, if her husband was unlucky enough to break a limb? These are extreme emergencies, but they could happen; and all sailing wives should bear them in mind, discuss them, and better still work out a plan of action for meeting them, and practice it.

This, of course, is looking on the very blackest side. More often than not the first aid kit is needed only for very minor troubles since the small family sailboat is not usually at sea long enough for more serious ailments to occur.

Lack of space, particularly in the galley, is the cause of many minor accidents below and it is here where a bit of forethought can reduce the risk of mishaps. Most likely are scalds and burns from the stove, and this is why the cook has supreme rights and right-of-way when she is busy in the galley. Sudden lurches as the ship moves make the likelihood of scalds from hot water, hot dishes and hot fat very real, and it is a good idea to wear waterproof trousers when cooking in a seaway, and boots too if the weather is really rough. Pans should never be more than half filled and the cook should always check to make sure the stove is free to swing and that the fiddles grip the pans securely. Oven gloves for juggling with hot pans are useful.

After one or two trips afloat and one or two minor accidents the cook soon knows what can go wrong and what steps she can take to guard against them. It becomes instinctive for her to check before opening back hatches and doors in case fingers are trapped, and to keep steps and entrances clear and dry so that they don't become skid traps; second nature to empty hot pans and kettles as soon as they come off the stove and before they can tip and scald the unwary. Most of the other accidents below are merely annoyances—bangs on knees, shins, elbows, head and so on, in the restricted space—which are all overcome as the art of living small is acquired.

Minor accidents, particularly finger-catching ones, are much more likely to happen on deck, but here again familiarity brings confidence; knowing the correct way to handle ropes, sheets, winches, anchors, engine, warps and lines is the criterion. Handled right, accidents hardly ever occur; handled wrongly the consequences can be very painful indeed. This is where good basic seamanship is the safeguard.

The sort of ailments likely to be encountered are headaches, stings, sore throats, toothache, septic spots, boils, food poisoning, eye troubles, sunburn, hay fever, constipation, colds, chills, seasickness, splinters, cuts, abrasions, burns, scalds, fainting, and so on; an impressive enough list, but the sort of troubles dealt with every day ashore and well within the scope of the first aid kit.

The first aid kit

The first aid kit might well start with the following, which can be altered and added to as time goes on. This is suggested as the very minimum to cope with the eventualities likely to arise.

Waterproof dressing	Hot water bottle	Sterilized dressings
Insect repellent	Burn dressings	Antidote to bites
Adhesive bandage	Cotton batting	Triangular bandage
Calamine	Aspirin	Suntan lotion
Boric acid	Finger stall	One-inch adhesive tape
Seasick tablets	Indigestion relief	Laxative
Antiseptic	Throat/mouth tablets	Antiseptic ointment
Eye lotion	Hay fever antidote	Eyewash
Scissors	Safety pins	Tweezer
Brandy	Thermometer	Paregoric
Lip salve	Toothache wax	Nail file

Choose a plastic box to keep the first aid equipment in, preferably an airtight one.

After the initial first aid treatment professional attention is needed for more serious accidents such as fractures, dislocations, deep cuts and gashes, serious burns, and high temperatures. Here are some suggested cures for troubles likely to be met.

Diarrhea. Half a teaspoon paregoric every six hours until symptoms cease.

Toothache (if due to cavity). Clean out with toothpick and cotton and pack with toothache wax. Aspirins will help.

Eyes. If foreign body cannot be removed easily leave it alone. Wash with eye lotion. If eye is really painful cover with pad and rest.

Food poisoning. Dilute as much as possible by swallowing large quantities of water. Induce vomiting by drinking salted water or tickling back of throat. Treat for shock, keep warm. Give hot tea or coffee. No solid food until patient is better.

Fainting. Sit with head between knees. Loosen clothing round neck. Treat for shock and give hot stimulants.

Shock. Lie down, head low. Wrap warmly, give hot tea/coffee providing there is no head injury or serious bleeding. Never give stimulants if patient is unconscious, but keep warm.

Sprains. Bathe in cold water for a good half hour. Dry and bind firmly, with elastic bandage. Rest the strained area.

Burns. Minor, no breaking of skin. Run under cold water to relieve pain. Apply burn dressing lightly.

More severe burns. Treat for shock. Burns which break skin must be kept moist. Use burn dressing and bandage lightly. Never prick blisters, never use oil. Get professional treatment as soon as possible.

Rope burns (caused by ropes running through hands). Extremely painful. Treat as heat burns.

Septic spots and boils. Apply hot fomentations of boric acid. Bandage lightly and repeat every three or four hours until there is no discharge. Then apply dry bandage.

Sunburn. In normal cases an application of calamine night and morning gives quick relief. Keep covered and away from sun's rays and use a protective cream before exposure to the sun again.

Dislocation. Dislocations need professional care as soon as possible. As a temporary relief cold may be applied to the joint but do not attempt to re-set. Support the limb in the most comfortable position, bound to the body or in a sling, and loosen clothing around the injury.

Fractures:

Toes. Leave alone.

Fingers. Apply small splint and fix in place with a bandage.

Small bones (feet or hands). Immobilize as far as possible with an elastic bandage.

Larger bones. Immobilize with splints or sling to prevent pain and shock. Professional attention as soon as possible.

Upset stomach. Keep warm. Dose with paregoric as directed. Warm drinks.

Small wounds. Small wounds which do not bleed readily should be washed with soap and water and then covered with sterilized dressing and bandaged. Keep well clear of salt water, which makes them sore and delays healing.

More serious cuts. Cuts which bleed heavily need thorough attention. Venous bleeding, which wells up in a slow, continous, dark red stream, can be stopped by a pad of sterilized gauze and a firm bandage over the wound, whereas arterial bleeding must be stopped by pressure, which is applied to the appropriate pressure point before dressing. If this is not sufficient a tourniquet may be needed. Remember that the tourniquet must be loosened every fifteen minutes, even if the bleeding starts again, otherwise more serious damage will result. Professional attention without delay.

Severe seasickness. Seasickness is the most common ailment of all afloat. Luckily for most of us it is a temporary malaise and it is only rarely that people become completely incapacitated. When they do they should get to bed and rest and keep warm; probably at this time the type of anti-sickness tablet which promotes drowsiness is best. Liquid intake should be kept to the minimum and dry crackers are the safest bet if food of some sort is needed.

A word or two about seasickness generally will not be out of place here. Remember, although seasickness is not an illness, it does cause acute depression and depression is contagious and a great lowerer of morale. The fact that going to sea and staying at sea may help to overcome seasickness, eventually, is no consolation to those in the initial stages of it. As mentioned earlier, careful feeding before going to sea and careful choice of food on board as well as anti-sickness tablets help to combat seasickness, but to my mind it is perfectly normal to be sick when a boat starts to jump about wildly at sea. The important thing is that people should realize there is no shame attached to feeling seasick and the worst thing they can do is try to hide the fact that they are. Seasickness gets worse as the sufferer becomes cold, tired and hungry; movement and action in the initial stages, which aids circulation, helps enormously.

Understanding on the part of the skipper and the rest of the crew goes a long way to helping the seasick face up to the fact that they are sick, but that there is a cure for it if it can only be found. If the normal remedies—tablets, keeping warm, drinking little, eating nothing but dry crackers—fail, the only real answer is to go below and try to get to sleep. This should be accomplished as quickly as ·possible, since the seasick sailor finds the motion below infinitely worse than on deck, but with the aid of an anti-sickness tablet this should not prove difficult. These tablets work particularly well with children and are an almost certain way of giving them rest when they need it most. On waking, a dry cracker or two nibbled before getting up ensures that the stomach is not completely empty, and once again no time should be wasted below. Fresh air above all else is needed now, and this is the time to keep interest alive and the circulation moving.

A lot of people swear they feel better once they have vomited; others strive to put off vomiting at all costs. There seems to be no general rule, but eventually, by trial and error, and after some very unhappy times, sufferers will find their own pet cures or preventives. What cures one may mean certain seasickness to another, but confidence is what matters most and this should be boosted at all costs.

The unfortunate thing is that everyone cannot turn in at once. Thus it is as well to know the crew's susceptibility in advance before setting out on a sea passage and ensure that at least one person is proof against seasickness.

A word of warning about the use of alcohol as a stimulant. Although brandy is listed among the contents of the first aid box and is an excellent booster if one has been thoroughly chilled, it should only be given to people going below to sleep or rest in the warm. Taken by anyone staying out in the cold it gives a quick, warm boost, but this is short-lived. The alcohol dilates the blood vessels under the skin, exposing the blood to the surrounding temperature; it also lowers efficiency, especially if the stomach is relatively empty.

No chapter on first aid and safety would be complete without some mention of artificial resuscitation. Anyone who goes to sea or, in fact, any visitor to the seashore, might be called upon to offer assistance of this sort at some time, and it's a wise precaution to have some idea what to do if an emergency should arise.

The expired air method (mouth to mouth or nose) is considered the most effective since it can be carried out by one person and produces better ventilation to the lungs than the manual methods. This is vitally important because lack of oxygen in the blood supply to the brain causes irreparable damage to the nerve cells in a matter of minutes. This is why resuscitation, whichever method is used, must be given as quickly as possible.

The following procedure may well save a life. For more complete information, write the American National Red Cross, 17th and D streets N.W., Washington, D.C. 20006.

How to carry out expired air resuscitation
1. Lay the patient on his back and, if on a slope, have the stomach slightly lower than the chest.
2. Make a brief inspection of the mouth and throat to ensure that they are clear of obvious obstruction.
3. Give the patient's head the maximum backwards tilt so that the chin is prominent, the mouth closed and the neck stretched to give clear airway.
4. Open your mouth wide, make an airtight seal over the nose of the patient and blow. The operator's cheek or the hand supporting the chin can be used to seal the patient's lips.
5. *Or,* if the nose is blocked, open the patient's mouth, using the hand supporting the chin, open your mouth wide and make an airtight seal over his mouth and blow. This may also be used as an alternative to the mouth-to-nose technique even when the nose is not blocked, in which case the nostrils must be sealed with the operator's cheek or the hand holding the top of the patient's head moved and the fingers used to pinch the nostrils. The wrist must be kept low on the patient's forehead to ensure that the full tilt of the head is maintained. If the patient's mouth cannot be opened, blow through his parted lips as the air passing between his teeth may be sufficient to inflate his lungs.

6. After exhaling, turn your head to watch for chest movement while inhaling deeply in readiness to blow again.

7. If the chest does not rise, check that the patient's mouth and throat are free of obstruction and the head is tilted backwards as far as possible. Blow again.

8. If air enters the patient's stomach through blowing too hard, press the stomach gently, with the head of the patient turned to one side.

9. Commence resuscitation with six quick inflations of the patient's chest to give a rapid build-up of oxygen in the patient's blood and then slow down to twelve to fifteen respirations per minute or blow again each time the patient's chest has deflated.

   With small children and babies, inflation at the rate of twenty a minute is achieved by a series of puffs, each one ceasing as the chest starts to rise. *Under no circumstances blow violently into a baby's lungs.*

10. While preparing to commence resuscitation breathe deeply with the mouth open to build up the oxygen content.

Sanitation afloat

Ventilation to the cabin cannot be too highly stressed. Remember, people live, eat, sleep, wash, and use the toilet in a very confined space, so cleanliness and good ventilation are essential. Ideally there should be a mushroom-type ventilator over the toilet and one over the galley as well, but in any case keep an air freshener near the toilet; it will help.

Salt water is an excellent disinfectant and luckily there's no shortage of it, so make certain the toilet is flushed out several times after use. The discharge pump to the toilet is very delicate. Don't mince words; make sure everybody on board knows just how delicate it is and spell out all the items which will block it and put it out of use for everybody. Better still, produce a list of do's and don'ts for the toilet and pin it up where it is in clear view. Even matches, hair, oddments of string, etc., will block the pump so if the toilet compartment is used for washing (and if it isn't it's probably a good idea to try to include a washbasin there, even if it's only a plastic bowl which empties into the toilet pan) beware of things like hairpins, toothpaste tops, razor blades, lipsticks, etc., getting into the pan. If they should, enlist the skipper's help— in no circumstances try to pump it through.

Being so delicate, the marine toilet cannot take heavy paper, disposable diapers, or cotton balls. This must be a hard and fast rule, and it will be up to the sea wife to make sure that every visitor on board knows it, too. Careful warning about using the toilet can guarantee a trouble-free life; carelessness can cause unlimited trouble and discomfort for all.

Glossary of Nautical Terms Used

ABAFT: behind or aft of

ABOARD: on board or in a vessel

ABOUT: go on the opposite tack

AGROUND: when the keel sits on the bottom

ALOFT: up the mast or in the rigging

AMIDSHIPS: in the center of the vessel, from bow to stern or across

ANCHOR ARM: one half of the curved part of a fisherman anchor

ANCHOR CHOCKS: special fittings on deck to which anchor is secured when not in use

ANCHOR FLUKE: part of the anchor which digs into the ground

ANCHOR LIGHT: lantern, showing white all round, which is hung in the fore rigging when vessel is at anchor

APPARENT WIND: the wind as experienced by a moving object as compared to a stationary one

BACKING (sails): hauling the clew of a sail to windward, which helps to turn the bow quickly

BACKSTAY: wire/rope leading aft from the mast to stop it bending forward

BALLAST KEEL: keel of iron or lead which gives stability as well as lateral resistance to the boat

BATTENS: stiffeners fitted in sail to stop leech flapping

BEAM: maximum breadth of vessel

BEAM REACHING: sailing at right angles to the wind

BEAM SEA: waves approaching the boat from the side

BEARING AWAY: putting the helm to windward to turn the vessel away from the wind

BEARINGS (by eye): direction of an object from where observer is standing

BEARINGS (compass): direction according to compass card

BEARINGS (transit): marks in line or range

BEATING: to tack; to sail a zigzag course upwind with wind first on one bow then the other

BENDING ON (sails): to fit sails to mast and spars ready for hoisting

BILGE: space in a vessel beneath the sole (the floor)

BOAT HOOK: staff with hook at one end for picking up moorings or floating objects

BOOM: horizontal spar for extending foot, or bottom, of sail

BOW: front of vessel

BROADSIDE ON: sideways on

BUNKS: sleeping berths

BUOY: floating marker for moorings, underwater obstructions, and channels

BUOYANCY BAGS: airtight bags fitted in dinghies in place of built-in tanks to give buoyancy if waterlogged

BURGEE: a swallow-tailed or triangular flag flown at masthead showing club to which owner belongs

CABIN TOP: part of the deck raised to give extra headroom

CABLE: anchor chain or rope

CAPSIZE: overturn, upset

CATAMARAN: twin-hulled vessel

CENTERBOARD: a central keel or plate which can be raised or lowered, usually pulled up for running and lowered to give lateral resistance when sailing closer to the wind

CHART DATUM: theoretical level from which height and depth are measured. Roughly the mean low tide level

CLEAT: wood or metal fitting to which rope may be secured without tying—usually by a round turn and figure of eight turns

CLEW (of sail): lower after-corner

CLOSE HAULED: sailing as close to the wind as possible

CLOSE REACH: point of sailing midway between reaching and close hauled

COCKPIT: well near the stern in which helmsman sits

COMPANIONWAY: entry from deck or the cockpit to the accommodation

COMPASS (bearing): direction according to compass card

COMPASS (course): directional heading taken from a bearing by magnetic compass

COMPASSES: instruments for maintaining direction or taking bearings. Magnetic compasses have a card with a magnetic north-seeking pole which is free to revolve in fluid

CRANE LINES: short tie-backs used to stop rigging tapping against mast

DECK HEAD: underside of deck

DEVIATION: compass error caused by nearby iron, etc., deflecting the north-seeking magnet from its alignment

DINGHY: ship's tender. Small open boat used for ferrying between vessel and shore

DISTRESS FLARES: pyrotechnic signals for summoning help in trouble

DOWN CURRENT: at a point from the observer in the direction to which the current is running

DOWN HAUL: rope for pulling down sails or boom

DRIFTING: moving with the tide or wind only

EBB TIDE: the dropping or receding tide

ECHO SOUNDER or FATHOMETER: electronic device for showing depth of water under vessel

ENSIGN: flag carried as insignia of nationality

EVEN KEEL: so trimmed as to float upright

FAIRLEAD: block or fitting through which a rope is passed to alter the direction of lead or keep it clear of fittings

FAIR TIDE: favorable tide; flowing in the same direction as the vessel

FATHOM: nautical measure of 6 feet

FENDERS (fendoffs): pads of rubber, rope, or cork for protecting the vessel when going alongside docks, or other vessels

FEND OFF: push off any obstruction which is liable to cause damage

FIDDLES: strips, usually wood, fitted to tables, ledges, etc., to stop things sliding off. Also metal or wood bars fitted to fixed stoves to keep pans securely in place

FITTING OUT: the yearly overhaul and spring-clean of a vessel before the start of the sailing season

FLOOD TIDE: rising tide

FO'C'SLE (forecastle): part of the accommodation beneath the foredeck

FOLLOWING SEA: waves going in the same direction as the vessel

FOOT (of sail): lower edge

FOREDECK: forward deck or front part of the deck over the fo'c'sle

FOREHATCH: deck access to the fo'c'sle

FORESAIL: headsail, usually hanked to the forestay

FORESTAY: wire/rope leading from bow to masthead

FOUL TIDE: unfavorable tide, going in opposite direction to the vessel

GALLEY: the ship's kitchen

GASH BIN: the ship's garbage can. Usually a bucket

GENOA: large triangular headsail for use in lighter winds

GIMBALS: system of keeping stove, lamp, compass, etc., swinging as boat moves so that it is always level

GOING ABOUT: altering course into the wind from one tack to the other

GRID COMPASS: magnetic steering compass fitted with movable ring which has parallel lines on it. The card has a corresponding line which must be kept in alignment

HALYARDS: ropes with which sails are hoisted

HAND-BEARING COMPASS: portable compass fitted with prism through which bearings of objects may be read by means of a sight

HANKS (or hanked): metal or plastic fittings by which sails are attached to masts or booms or hoisted up stays

HARDEN IN (sails): haul in sheets to flatten sails

HEAD: the marine toilet, so called because it is usually right up in the bow (or head) of the ship

HEAD (of sail): top corner of sail which is hoisted up mast or stay

HEADING UP: turning bow of vessel nearer to the wind

HEADROOM: distance in vessel between cabin sole and deckhead

HEADSAILS: triangular sails set forward of the mast

HEAD SEA: waves coming from the direction in which it is desired to sail

HEAD TO WIND: vessel facing directly into the wind

HEADWAY: forward progress of vessel through the water

HEAD WIND: wind blowing from the direction in which it is desired to sail

HEAVE TO: trim helm and sails so that vessel remains almost stationary

HEAVING LINE: light line, usually with knob on end, thrown to make contact between vessel and the shore when going alongside, etc.

HEEL: a boat's leaning over

HELM: tiller or wheel used for steering. Tiller usually a metal or wooden bar fitted to the rudder head

HIGH WATER: the time at which a flood tide reaches its highest point

HOISTING: raising, lifting sails

HULL: body of the vessel, excluding masts and gear

JIB: headsail set forward of the fore staysail

JIBE: transfer mainsail from one side of the ship to the other when running

KNOT: measure of speed. One knot = one nautical mile per hour = 6080 feet per hour

LASHED DOWN: tied down securely

LATITUDE: distance north or south of the Equator, expressed in degrees

LAYING UP: storing boat for the winter, afloat, in mud berth or ashore

LEAD LINE: weight on marked line used to find depth of water

LEECH (of sail): aftermost edge of sail

LEE SIDE: side opposite to that on which wind is blowing

LEEWARD: any point downwind of the observer or an object

LIFEBUOY: circular or horseshoe-shaped float, kapok- or cork-filled and usually big enough to encircle a man's chest

LIFELINES: rope or wire passed through uprights along the side of the vessel's deck to prevent crew falling overboard

LIFE RAILS or PULPITS: form of safety fence around the deck

LONGITUDE: distance in degrees east or west of the meridian of Greenwich

LOW WATER: lowest point of the tide

LUBBER LINE: mark on the compass bowl which corresponds with the ship's head

LUFF (of sail): forward part of sail

LUFFING: bringing vessel so close to the wind that sails start to flutter

MAGNETIC NORTH: direction in which magnetic North Pole at present lies

MAINSAIL: the principal sail

MAKE FAST: to secure a rope

MAST: a spar set upright on deck to support rigging and sails

MERIDIAN: a true north and south line

MOORING: permanent anchoring equipment laid on the seabed to keep vessel floating in one position

MULTIHULL: vessel with more than one hull

NEAP TIDES: tides which rise and fall least. Opposite to spring tides

PAINTER: rope attached to bow of dinghy by which it is towed along or secured to vessel, dock, etc.

PARALLEL RULES: rules, used in navigation, designed so that they can be moved around on the chart with the edges always parallel

PORT: left side of the ship looking forward. Signified by red light. Opposite to starboard

PORT TACK: sailing close hauled with wind blowing over the port side

QUARTER: part of the vessel midway from abeam to astern to the stern. Thus either port or starboard quarter
QUARTER BERTH: bunk running under the side of the cockpit

REACHING: see "beam reaching"
REEFING: reducing the size of the sail, usually by rolling it round the boom
RIDING LIGHT: all-round white light shown when at anchor
RIGGING (running): halyards for hoisting sails, sheets for trimming sails, etc.
RIGGING (standing): wire and/or rope used to support mast and spars
RUDDER: blade fitted at stern by which vessel is steered

SAFETY HARNESS: webbing harness with line and snap-hook attached to minimize the risk of falling overboard
SAIL AREA: square measurement of sails
SALOON: main living space in vessel
SCOPE: length of cable by which vessel is anchored
SEACOCK: taps for shutting off pipes which pass through the hull
SEA MILES: one nautical mile = approx. 1.15 land miles
SEAWAY: exposed and broken water
SEIZING END: to secure or to bind ends of ropes or two parts of the same rope together
SETTING (sails): hoisting sails ready for sailing
SHEETS: rope attached to the clew of a sail by which it is controlled
SLACK TIDE: short period at turn of the tide when there is no tidal stream
SNUBBING (anchor): stopping the chain running suddenly so that it jerks
SOUNDING: measuring depth of water under the vessel
SPAR: stunt wood or metal member used to support rigging
SPILL WIND: to turn closer to wind or to slack the sheet so that the wind is shaken out of the sails

SPINNAKER: large parachute-like triangular sail of light fabric used for running and reaching

SPLICES: method for joining ropes permanently or forming eyes in them

SPRING TIDES: those which rise and fall most. Opposite to neap tides

STANCHIONS: posts fitted round the deck to hold lifelines

STARBOARD: right hand side of vessel when looking forward. Signified by green light. Opposite to port

STARBOARD TACK: sailing close hauled with wind blowing over the starboard side

STEERING BY COMPASS: maintaining a course by keeping the compass card on a selected heading

STERN: back of vessel

STOWING (sails): taking sails down, right off the spars

TACKS, TACKING: beating to windward in a zigzag manner with wind first on one bow then the other

TACK, TACKLE: block (pulley) attached to the luff of a sail which allows it to be pulled taut

TENDER: a yacht's dinghy

THREE POINT BEARING: the intersection of three bearings (usually by compass) giving a positive position when plotted on the chart

TIDAL RANGE: the distance which the level of the water travels between low water and the succeeding high water

TIDES: rise and fall of the sea under the influence of the moon and sun

TIDE TABLES: tables showing tidal predictions for the year. These include times of high water and heights of tides

TIDEWAY: the actual stream of the tide

TILLER: wood or metal bar secured to the rudder head by means of which vessel is steered

TOPPING LIFT: wire or rope supporting outer end of boom

TRIMARAN: three-hulled vessel

TRIMMING SAILS: pulling sails in or letting them out so that they draw to the best advantage

TROUGH (weather): a low-pressure system usually giving a short time of bad, or dull, weather

TRUE NORTH: direction in which geographical north lies

TRUE WIND: the wind as it is felt by a stationary observer

TWIN KEELS: a boat having two ballast keels placed side by side instead of one central keel

UNDER WAY: a vessel is under way when it moves over the ground or through the water

UP CURRENT: at a point from the observer in the direction from which the current is running

WARPS: strong rope used for securing alongside, mooring, or towing

WEATHER SIDE: side of vessel on which wind is blowing. Opposite to lee side

WHIPPING: binding the end of a rope to stop it coming unraveled

WINCH: a revolving drum which gives extra power for handling ropes

WINDAGE: the above-water hull and superstructure which offers resistance to the wind

WINDWARD: direction from which wind is blowing

Index

Dinghy, handling of, 38-39,
41, 53, 91, 122-123
Dishes, pots, and pans
choice of, 17
stowage of, 31
Distress signals, 120-121

Emergencies, 112-121. *See
also* First aid
Engine controls, 68
Equipment, choice of, 17-22,
35-37

Family sailing, 147-164. *See
also* Routines
Fatigue, 28
Feeding at sea, 136-146. *See
also* Food; Recipes
Fenders, handling of, 88-89,
92
Fire and fire extinguishers,
37, 112-114
First aid, 175-182
Fitting out, 123-128
Food
supplies on board, 129-131
to avoid seasickness, 11
to stave off fatigue, 28-30
See also Cooking; Recipes

Galleys, 14
choosing stove for, 35-37
outfitting of, 17, 21-22
planning of, 30-32

Gimbals, 35

Halyards, making fast, 64
Heaving line, 80-83
Helmsmanship, 65-68. *See
also* Navigation
Hitches, knots, and bends.
See Knots

Jib, backing the, 55-56
Jibing, 43, 49, 58

Knots, hitches, and bends,
83-86

Leadline, 86-88
Life ring. *See*
Man-overboard procedure
Lifejackets. *See* Buoyancy
aids
Lighting equipment, 19-20
Lights carried by ships,
94-96
Liquor. *See* Alcohol
Lockers, 22
Luffing up, 47, 49

Maintenance work. *See*
Fitting out
Man-overboard procedure,
114-120
Menu planning, 130-135
Mooring, 52-58, 80-83